"*Fire Child, Water Child* is a breakthrough work. Children are unique and deserve an expanded and elevated approach to healing. This stunning book points toward complementary and healthy alternatives to pharmaceutical remedies."

> —Deepak Chopra, MD, author and cofounder of the
> Chopra Center for Wellbeing

"'Not a disease, but a symptom,' is Dr. Cowan's stunningly insightful summation of ADHD. *Fire Child, Water Child* offers a deep understanding of the types of children who may manifest attention difficulties. Dr. Cowan identifies what is right about them, innate positive qualities we can support to promote their development. Far more compassionate than the standard narrow medical approach, this book is also more scientific in its appreciation of children's relationship to their environment."

> —Gabor Maté, MD, author of *Scattered: How Attention Deficit
> Disorder Originates and What You Can Do About It*

"Stephen Scott Cowan's clinical skill and experience is unrivaled. His original approach has helped hundreds of children. Read and heed the wisdom embedded in his work."

> —Frank Lipman, MD, author of *Revive: Stop Feeling Spent
> and Start Living Again*

D1057188

"Dr. Cowan has written an exceptionally thoughtful, repercussive book that will surely change the lives of children and parents looking for profound, holistic ways to understand and heal attention-deficit hyperactivity disorder (ADHD). Not only has he created a masterful treatise in which children's root natures are brought to light as key ingredients in their bespoke recoveries, but he has also contributed a beautifully crafted ode to rebuilding attention. Dr. Cowan's support and recommendations have indeed proven transformative for me and for my son, Water child extraordinaire. This unique and brilliant book is a tour-de-force and finally, blessedly, reveals Dr. Cowan's gentle genius to the world."

—Maggie Lyon, writer on wellness and spirituality, holistic lifestyle consultant, and founder of lyonlifestyle.com

"This is such a good book—as practical as it is poetic. Dr. Cowan helps us to know our anxious, troubled, and sometimes troubling kids in new, more appreciative, and more compassionate ways. He teaches us that ADHD is as varied as the children who show its symptoms. In helping us adults step-by-step to help them, he helps us grow in love as well as knowledge."

—James S. Gordon, MD, psychiatrist, founder of The Center for Mind Body Medicine, and author of *Unstuck: Your Guide to the Seven-Stage Journey Out of Depression*

"I was deeply fortunate to have Dr. Cowan as our devoted and honorable pediatrician. His passionate and essential life's work is expressed beautifully and accessibly on these pages and profoundly serves to revolutionize, demystify, and guide families lost in the ambiguities of ADHD/ADD; pharmaceuticals; the cultural divide; and diversities of treatments, awareness, and balance. This book is a critical tool parents can use to support their children and encourage them to find a home within themselves, a precious gift."

—Paulette Cole, CEO and creative director of ABC Home in New York, NY

"Cowan empowers us to see beyond generic labels that lead to one-size-fits-all thinking. He offers dazzling insights into the nature of each individual child, potentially revolutionizing how children are cared for by their families, educated by their teachers, and treated by their physicians."

—Harriet Beinfield, coauthor of *Between Heaven and Earth*

"This is an extraordinary addition to the literature on childhood developmental disorders. Every parent and clinician treating this complex set of problems needs to read this book. Dr. Cowan has taken his thorough knowledge of medical science and decades of personal experience in studying and treating ADD and other developmental disorders, then combined them in an amazing synthesis with the energetic principles and characteristics of imbalance given to us by traditional Chinese medicine. This allows a broader, deeper and more individual understanding of each person's unique problems and needs, allowing a much better chance of success in producing lasting transformations. Brilliant."

—Woodson Merrell, MD, chairman of the department of integrative medicine at Beth Israel Medical Center in New York, NY, and author of *Power Up*

"Dr. Cowan's *Fire Child, Water Child* is a breath of fresh air in the current world of ADD and ADHD literature. He combines his true healer's motivation, years of successful practice, sound modern medical knowledge, and sane judgment derived from serious study of time-tested Asian medical wisdom to present us with a new way of seeing ADHD. His method encourages us to look at kids as the wondrous individuals that they are, care for them one by one in a truly human way, and save them and their parents from deep angst. As a dad and a granddad, I love this book and recommend it highly to everyone who loves their kids and wants to make sure that they thrive against whatever odds they face."

—Robert Thurman, father, grandfather, great-grandfather, and professor of Tibetan Buddhist studies at Columbia University

fire child
water child

how understanding the
five types of ADHD can help you improve
your child's self-esteem & attention

Stephen Scott Cowan, MD

New Harbinger Publications, Inc.

Publisher's Note

NEW HARBINGER PUBLICATIONS is a registered trademark of
New Harbinger Publications, Inc.

Distributed in Canada by Raincoast Books

Copyright © 2012 by Stephen Scott Cowan
                New Harbinger Publications, Inc.
                5674 Shattuck Avenue
                Oakland, CA 94609
                www.newharbinger.com

Cover design by Amy Shoup
Text design by Tracy Carlson
Acquired by Jess O'Brien
Edited by Carole Honeychurch

Library of Congress Cataloging-in-Publication Data

Cowan, Stephen Scott.
  Fire child, water child : how understanding the five types of ADHD can help you improve your child's self-esteem and attention / Stephen Scott Cowan.
    p. cm.
  Includes bibliographical references.
  ISBN 978-1-60882-090-0 (pbk.) -- ISBN 978-1-60882-091-7 (pdf e-book) -- ISBN 978-1-60882-092-4 (epub)
  1. Attention-deficit hyperactivity disorder--Psychological aspects. 2. Attention-deficit-disordered children--Psychology. 3. Attention-deficit hyperactivity disorder. I. Title.
  RJ506.H9C69 2012
  618.92'8589--dc23   2011044085

Printed in the United States of America

23   22   21

15   14   13   12   11   10

Contents

Foreword

Parents of an ADD/ADHD-identified child are often led to believe that there's something neurologically wrong with their child's brain. The child, confounded by impulses and actions out of sync with prevailing standards and expectations, is labeled as pathological. Reacting to an ominous judgment, fraught parents are plunged into a quagmire of conflicting opinions— medical, educational, social, and even moral. They are urged to make agonizing choices about brain- and mind-altering pharmaceuticals with side effects and unknown long-term consequences. Then there's the daunting task of sorting through a panoply of adjunctive therapies including dietary changes to address potential food sensitivities, the use of nutritional supplements, and cognitive and learning interventions.

Dr. Stephen Cowan, a gifted neurodevelopmental pediatrician, was dissatisfied after treating thousands of children over three decades. In response, he created an innovative model that deconstructs, demystifies, and reframes ADD/ADHD. In this book he provides a method for comprehensively evaluating *who the individual child is* that has been given the label ADD/ADHD.

Cowan paints pictures of five types of children who manifest five different types of ADD/ADHD. Each child has an intrinsic organizing pattern, a true nature, known as that child's *type*. Each type shares the agency of one of the five primal powers described in Chinese medicine as Wood, Fire, Earth, Metal, and Water. One of these five powers functions as the governing center that is the source of a child's predispositions, organizing how her experience is received, incorporated, and expressed.

Identifying children by their type provides insight into how they are likely to function within themselves and in their world. In this model, type defines the dynamic pattern that shapes us from birth to old age—it is the ontological matrix out of which each unique life forms itself.

Cowan's elastic framework articulates a coherent account of the causes and diagnosis of this perplexing syndrome. Informed by the observed features of each child according to type, he offers tailored treatment approaches. Identifying a child's type provides a template for predicting future challenges, enabling the prevention of minor problems from morphing into serious, chronic disorders.

Cowan's father inducted him as a young boy into an apprenticeship as an artist. Painting excursions into the New England woods inculcated an appreciation for the details, patterns, and rhythms in nature, a paradigm that became the foundation of his thinking and worldview. His training as a physician, coupled with years of careful observation, enabled him to evaluate what worked and what didn't, what made sense and what did not. He sought out Chinese medicine and Daoist philosophy to deepen his understanding of human life and expand the scope of his medical knowledge. We developed a collaboration in the early 1990s to build bridges between Chinese medicine and Western pediatrics.

Cowan has a scholar's insatiable curiosity about the fundamental nature of life, a clinician's determination to help individual children, and an artist's talent for formulating a radically new approach. This system is effective not only in treating ADD/ADHD, but also for tackling the entire spectrum of neurodevelopmental disorders. As student, teacher, doctor, artist, and healer, Cowan generously shares his knowledge, experience, compassion, acumen, and ingenuity here. Parents, teachers, physicians, researchers, the young, and the curious all will gain fresh insights and stratagems as they mine the valuable ore contained within these pages.

—Efrem Korngold, OMD, LAc
　Coauthor, *Between Heaven and Earth: A Guide to Chinese Medicine*
　Spring, 2011, Salmon River, Klamath National Forest

Acknowledgments

Any book is a child. It has its own unique conception, born of intentions whose roots are watered by many sources. This book would not be possible without the inspiration of my twin Fire brothers: Frank Lipman and Larry Baskind. Larry, for giving me the courage to step outside the box, and Frankie, for making sure I stay there. Of course, this child could never have grown past infancy without the nourishment of kindness and wisdom from my mentors, Harriet Beinfield and Efrem Korngold, who have kept my head nodding yes ever since I sat in their workshop eighteen years ago. The muscle and tendons of this book have been regularly exercised by the vast community of practitioners whose paths I've thankfully crossed through the years. To name but a few: Steven Aung, Thea Elijah, Nan Lu, Ed Young, Ken Cohen, Geri Brewster, and Woody Merrell. The bones of this book grew from the support of Robert Thurman, whose Menla Mountain House helped me bring the first draft to light. Its marrow is enriched by the warmth of my dear sister Jill and brother-in-friend Dan, whose TideWinds is where this book found its completion. The body of this work has been sustained by my family: Ben and Kate, Reggie and Peter, Nancy, Janelle, and boy Jamie. The flesh of this project could not exist without the countless children who are my constant teachers and their parents, whose questions make this life my path. The skin of this child owes a sincere debt of gratitude to Jess O'Brien and Carole Honeychurch at New Harbinger, the staff at Riverside Pediatrics, and the many friends whose patience has allowed the book to take shape organically—a rare thing these days. To the lights of my life, Sarah and Emily, who have kept the lifeblood in these pages circulating with their qi. To George and Trudi, who are the sky and earth watching over me, may they smile at this small feat. But the heart of this book beats with the laughter and love of my beloved Susan, without whom I would surely be cast adrift without a hand to hold in this crazy, topsy-turvy world. May this book learn to walk on its own and travel long and far in its life.

Introduction

Mapping a Path
to Attention

"ADHD is a symptom, not a disease." Each time I say these words to parents I can sense their confusion. "What's the difference?" they ask. Symptom or disease, my child still has a problem." Yes, having trouble paying attention *is* a real problem, but it doesn't mean there's something wrong with your child. It doesn't mean that something is broken in your child's brain that needs fixing. Words like "wrong," "broken," and "fixing" carry with them the burden of deep judgment, guilt, and fear. This book is not about fear. It is about developing a sense of compassion for the diverse ways in which we engage with the world and recognizing the qualities each child has to offer.

A Teacher Who Made a Difference

In 1966, the Beatles were experimenting with new sounds, the civil rights movement was breaking down old barriers, and for the first time we were stepping off the planet into the unknown of space. It was an exciting time to be alive. I was in sixth grade, spending much of my time staring out the window or drawing doodles in the margins of my schoolwork. If I happened to draw something funny, the kids around me would laugh. This would invariably get me singled out by the teacher, who would make me pay for my disruption of the class. Extra homework. Staying after school. I knew the drill well. In my doodles there were new and curious designs to be discovered. Out the window, the trees waved on in the wind. There was poetry there. And in making kids laugh there was a certain, albeit irreverent, wit.

Things had gone from bad to worse by fifth grade. I'd been tested by the school psychologists because of my poor focus. If you had asked me back then why I went to school, I would have answered like many of the kids I see today: "Because I have to." This all culminated one morning when I absentmindedly walked into a wall in my classroom that was covered with my teacher's cherished photographs of past classes, causing them to come crashing down.

But I was one of the lucky ones. That year I had a teacher, Miss Baggerman, who was to be one of a series of saviors in my life. What she did then was so simple yet so profound that I have never forgotten it. While the class looked on in horror, she sternly told me to come to her desk and stand there as she wrote a letter, *in red ink*, that I was to take home to my parents. She told me not to read the letter, knowing full well that as soon as I left the classroom I would open it and read it. It said that there was a problem, that "Stephen does not know how to walk in class," and that my parents were to come in to speak with her as soon as possible. I was to accompany them. That was it. It said nothing else. Now, I was a real schemer. I thought of not showing the letter to them, of hiding it in the chaos of clutter in my room and then claiming I had forgotten about it. I thought of dropping it in a puddle so that it couldn't be read. But most of all, I thought that the problem would simply disappear with time. But something compelled me to show it to my parents. I'm not sure what it was. Maybe it was the way she handed it to me with such authority. Was I going to be kicked out of the school? Was I going to be punished in some unimaginable way?

I went home and watched my mother's expression turn as she read the letter. Tears were in her eyes. "I didn't *mean* to do it," I tried desperately to explain. That night I nervously waited for my father's explosion of disappointment. But it never came. Before bed we had one of our big family meetings. I was asked why the teacher said I don't know how to walk in class, but I couldn't answer. As my parents sat on my bed with me, they spoke quietly and said we'd have to see what Miss Baggerman had planned for me the next day.

That was a long, restless night and an even longer walk to school than usual the next morning. There seemed to be no way out of this mess. During school, Miss Baggerman gave no hint of what she had in store for me. I began to think the problem might just go away after all. But when the afternoon bell rang and all the kids went flying out the door, I saw both my parents standing in the hall. My father, having had to leave early from work, was looking very serious. This, paired with my mother's sympathetic smile of concern, had me fighting to hold back my tears. As the noise faded, Miss Baggerman asked my parents to sit down at her desk, which seemed to have grown to the size of a small hippopotamus. She proceeded to show them the wall with the broken picture frames. She asked about the past few years when I had gotten in trouble for not paying attention in class. She then went through my desk and showed them my doodles. One was a pretty good caricature of her looking like Woodrow Wilson. I looked to my father for a sign of his typical humor but there was none. She then told them that I wouldn't be passing this year unless something drastic was done. I was disrespectful and a daydreamer, and she would not allow this in her classroom. Then she said something that would change everything. She said that she believed there was a bright boy in there somewhere, and she asked my parents' permission to "do whatever it takes" to get me to perform my best.

There was a long silence. "What do you mean, 'whatever it takes'?" my father asked. "You're not going to beat him, are you?" My father had been raised in England in the 1920s, where beatings were a regular occurrence, and he certainly didn't approve of this. I gulped. "I don't know yet," Miss Baggerman said, looking directly at me. My eyes widened. I was trying to motion to my folks, "Say no! Say no way!" but they weren't looking at me. They stared directly at the teacher's determined, controlled expression. My mother then turned to my father and looked deeply into his eyes without saying a word. I couldn't figure out what they were thinking. I couldn't figure out what anyone was talking about here. This was crazy! Finally the long silence was broken by my father clearing his voice and saying, "If you think you can help my son, I will trust you." All Miss Baggerman said in reply was, "We have to try."

And without another word, we left.

The Baggerman Tactic

What she did from that day on was quite remarkable. There was never any discussion of labels or diseases or medication, although if medication had been as accessible as it is today I'm sure I would have been a prime candidate for some prescription. What she did was sit me right in front of her in the classroom. She then proceeded to call on me first for *every single question* she asked the class. Day in, day out. For weeks and then for months. At first it was clear just how "tuned out" I was. I had no idea *how* to pay attention in class. The other children would laugh at me when I had no idea what the teacher was talking about, but she would simply move on to someone else. After a few weeks of this, I became increasingly embarrassed and annoyed. But Miss Baggerman remained in complete control of her emotions and the class. If she was feeling angry or frustrated, she certainly didn't show it, nor did she show any sign of wavering in her intentions. She was not going to give up on me. I tried any way I could to change her determination. I tried being cute; that didn't work. I tried being sorry; that didn't work. I tried sulking, getting angry, and ignoring her, but nothing worked. Finally, after weeks and weeks of this, something shifted. One day, she asked a question and, knowing that I was going to be picked to answer first, I listened very carefully and answered correctly. And Miss Baggerman smiled. It was the first time I had ever noticed her smile. It was fleeting but directed straight at me. She then moved on to another kid. A strange sensation came over me. Was this what paying attention in class was all about? Did I just have to follow what she was saying? Thoroughly engaged, I waited for the next question to come around and, sure enough, I got it right. She smiled again! I remember that smile like it was yesterday. It was that brief smile that filled me with such a sense of accomplishment. As the days went on, I began getting every question correct and it started showing in my grades. I still hated doing homework, but it somehow *mattered* more. It mattered to my teacher. Within a few months I was at the top of my class, and suddenly a different group of kids wanted to be my friends. Now when my parents asked how my day had been, I had important things to talk about rather than just saying "Fine" (my usual answer for everything until then). Miss Baggerman had taken me under her wing. In time she began suggesting a few books for me to read, in particular biographies. A book on the life of Thomas Edison was a particular favorite. So was one on Anton van

Leeuwenhoek, the inventor of the microscope (whose name I took particular pleasure in saying with a Dutch accent).

While I would go on to have other challenges in the years to come, this was the taste of some kind of validation of who I was, of experiencing a new kind of attention, one in which I was tuning in to something bigger than my small, self-centered world. Tuned in, I suddenly cared what my teacher thought of me. Tuned in, I cared about my grades. Tuned in, I cared about learning new things. And, as a result, there were whole new worlds to explore.

What Miss Baggerman had done was to carefully, gradually, bring me back in tune with the world. Doing that might seem impossible for a teacher now. She would be fired on the spot for even hinting at laying a hand on a student, and I'm certainly not suggesting that is a solution to any problem. And what teacher now has the time to spend on one child like Miss Baggerman did with me? All too often I hear teachers say, "If I did that for Johnny I'd have to do it for every kid in the class." Now, I'm not suggesting that this is all you have to do for children to get them to pay attention. In fact, that's the point of this book. Miss Baggerman took the time to know whom she was dealing with and responded in kind. There are different solutions for different children. But this all begins with knowing what kind of child you have.

Different Approaches for Different People

My own path mirrors the ways I have been able to help thousands of children with ADHD. Miss Baggerman was a beginning, but it took me years to discover *how I learn*. We assume children all learn the same way, but this simply isn't true. That is what this book is actually about. For me, it took being in medical school to realize that learning how to pay attention was a matter of life and death. I had to stop trying to learn the way my roommates did and figure out the way that worked best for me. I began by asking myself how information actually got into my brain. This is the first question I ask every child I meet who is struggling to learn. For me, it just so happens that I learn by context and pictures and maps. Even back in Miss Baggerman's class, those doodles were an important clue. I have always had a talent for painting and drawing and remembering images. It just comes naturally. In college I struggled in class to listen, but if there was a picture I could understand the information perfectly and remember it. I was a visual learner caught in an auditory world. Up in my attic to this day, there are shoeboxes filled with little index cards that contain diagrams with pictures and arrows and hieroglyphics I'd invented that helped me map out all the anatomy and pathology I had to learn in medical school. While it was work to make them, it was actually fun. By the time I was an intern in a hospital, I became a star on rounds because I could see all those connections in my mind while others were thinking about what page the answer might be on. The discovery that there are different ways of learning would inspire me to specialize in child development.

Later, while working as a developmental pediatrician, I became increasingly frustrated. The system I was trained in seems to leave the child out of the equation, labeling symptoms as the problem and condemning children to a life of medication. I began searching for a more holistic picture of health. This led me to meet Harriet Beinfield and Efrem Korngold, the authors of *Between Heaven and Earth* (1992). They were the first teachers to show me a new way of mapping health according to the principles of Chinese medicine. This resonated perfectly with the way I understood children. Chinese medicine honors our diversity, speaking in relatives rather than absolutes, and thus avoids reducing us to mere labels. Over these past fifteen years of study, I have seen time and time again the amazing ways that the forces of nature (water, wood, fire, earth, and metal) shape our lives. By applying these principles to child development, I've found a map that has helped thousands of children improve their attention.

In fact, I've created this book as a kind of map to help you navigate your way to your own child's strengths. In chapter 1, you will learn what the problems are with the diagnosis of attention deficit/hyperactivity disorder (ADHD) and why it seems to be a modern epidemic. In chapter 2, you will discover the important links between stress and attention. What I call *holistic developmental pediatrics* is really just taking a larger view of all the forces at play in your child's life. In particular, we'll be looking at what supports a sense of security and what is undermining it. In chapter 3, we will take a closer look at "The Three Treasures," how we use our brains to focus. This is the first step in truly understanding attention. We'll go even deeper in chapter 4, discovering the five different ways children pay attention and the ways they lose focus. This tailored focus lies at the heart of what makes this book unique. Most books about ADHD tend to make general assumptions and recommendations that ignore the unique nature of each child.

This book is dedicated to all those children who seem to be struggling to fit in and to those parents who are seeking deeper ways of understanding the child they love and effective methods to help her become a true master of attention. It is my hope that after reading this book you will be able to see beyond the diagnosis and recognize the dynamic ways in which your child can find the freedom to pay attention.

Chapter 1

Problems with the Diagnosis of ADHD

A wise man guards his attention as his most precious possession.

Dhammapada 26

Malcolm is brought to my office by his father, who is demanding Malcolm be tested for ADHD. "There's something wrong with my child," he says. "How is it I manage to wake up in the morning on my own, get dressed, eat breakfast, get to work on time, and put in a full day's work, and he can't even seem to get his shoes on in the morning?" Malcolm, meanwhile, is sitting quietly staring out the window, wondering when this is going to be over so he can get home in time to finish building his Lego starship.

For thousands of years children have been learning in natural ways. A child's innate talents would lead him to be chosen as someone's apprentice. He would watch the master work and then try it himself. It is only in the past hundred years that we have put children in a classroom and expected them to all learn by listening in exactly the same way. Out of necessity we have created standards by which we can guarantee education as a right for all children. This has been a wonderful way to expose children to all kinds of information that they would otherwise not have had access to, but it also has a downside. How can we expect all children to pay attention in the same way? This is a little like expecting all tomato plants to grow identically. Eminent researchers like Howard Gardner have done pioneering work describing the diverse ways we learn, and yet we continue to place children in the same box. And the smaller the box gets, the more children fall out of it.

The Epidemic of ADHD

Attention deficit/hyperactivity disorder is defined by the American Psychiatric Association as the inability to pay attention, manifesting as some combination of distractibility, impulsivity, and sometimes hyperactivity (2000). While we do not know the exact number of children diagnosed with ADHD, it has certainly been rising at a rapid rate. According to the Centers for Disease Control and Prevention, in 2007 it was estimated that as many as 9.5 percent of all school-age children in the United States were currently or had been medicated because they couldn't pay attention. The percentage of children being diagnosed rose on average each year from 2003 and 2007 by 5.5 percent (2010). There is no evidence that this rate of increase is leveling off. Extrapolating these numbers, the rate of ADHD in 2011 can be estimated to be as high as 15 percent. That makes ADHD the most common psychiatric diagnosis, with at least 10 million children having been diagnosed at the time of this writing. That's a big number. It rivals the number of people diagnosed with heart disease in the United States. That makes ADHD just as much an epidemic as cardiac disease.

Or does it? While the diagnosis is certainly rising, it's unclear whether more children are actually having problems with their attention or whether more labels are being handed out. Let's look for a moment at how the diagnosis is made.

Circular Logic: The Myth of Diagnosis

Every day I hear stories like Malcolm's in my office. Parents come in wanting their child "tested for ADHD" because the teacher tells them the child is struggling. I respond by telling these parents: *There is no test for ADHD.* Parents look shocked when they learn this. The idea that there is some sort of definitive, scientific test for this disorder may be one of the biggest myths in medicine. What we do have is a kind of circular logic in evaluating children for ADHD that may actually be fueling the epidemic. Here's how it typically works:

1. A teacher observes that a child is not paying attention in the classroom.

2. She alerts the parents that something may be wrong with the child and they then bring their child to a doctor.

3. The doctor then gives the parents a questionnaire to be filled out by the teacher.

4. The teacher, who has already decided that the child has a problem, then fills out the questionnaire. She checks off all the boxes that confirm that the child is having trouble paying attention and returns the form to the doctor.

5. The doctor then looks at the so-called evidence and makes the diagnosis of ADHD.

6. Once the diagnosis is made, it's simply a matter of prescribing the medicine for the diagnosis.

There are several problems with this approach. For one, it begins with an assumption. That assumption is that every teacher has the same experience evaluating attention in children. It does not consider how long a teacher has been working with children or whom she is comparing a child to. Nor does the questionnaire account for teacher bias. In fact it tells me more about a teacher's expectations of what a child should *look* like when he or she is paying attention than it does about the child. And even this is completely subjective. What "fidgety" means to one teacher may not be the same for another. What's more, there is no way of knowing whether the teacher's responses are based on her memory of the child's behavior over a period of time or based on observations on a particular day.

More importantly, the questionnaire makes no attempt at understanding the context in which the child is supposed to be paying attention. It doesn't tell me how the schoolwork is being presented, who's sitting next to the child, how much sleep the child got that day, or what he had to eat for breakfast. I could put you in a room and make you read one of my old physics books and you might seem to have ADHD, based on the questionnaire. What's more worrisome, these results are taken as all the evidence a doctor needs to prescribe medication for a child.

Interestingly, boys are diagnosed with ADHD far more often than girls are. This has always made me a little suspicious about the whole diagnostic process. Why would boys outnumber girls in attention problems? This imbalance has led many experts to assume that ADHD is fundamentally a genetic disorder, that boys are somehow genetically programmed to have trouble focusing. But then why would the number of children with ADHD be rising? Genetic disorders never happen in epidemics. So if it's not genetic, then the environment must be playing a role in the rise in diagnoses. Even if we ignore the fact that the statistics are based on biased evidence, the questionnaire still tells us nothing about the environment.

Another worrisome trend in the past decade has been the abrupt rise in the diagnosis of ADHD in preschool-age children (Zito et al. 2000). Using a questionnaire originally intended for older children has led to the increasing "off-label" use of stimulant medications in children much younger than the drug companies' testing population. *Off label* simply means that the drug is being used without FDA approval or research. There are no long-term studies on the safety of these medications in such young children.

Now, it's certainly true that a teacher is in a difficult situation when a child is distracted in her class. We know that, if left untreated, children with ADHD are at increased risk for developing chronic low self-esteem that can lead to lifelong problems with depression, anxiety, failed relationships, unemployment, substance abuse, antisocial behavior, and other dangerous risk-taking behaviors (Mannuzza et al. 2004). So what is really going on here?

ADHD Is Like Fever

ADHD is a cry for help. In that way, it's like fever. But fever is not a disease. This is an important distinction. Many people think a diagnosis is the same thing as a disease. But it's not. This is especially true when it comes to developmental diagnoses like ADHD. It's important to realize that we are simply giving a label to a cluster of symptoms. Treating symptoms is very different from treating a disease. The diagnosis of a disease like strep throat or diabetes tells us the cause and implies that there is a specific way to fix the problem. A symptom, however, is merely an expression of an underlying problem. In that way it is like an alert. There may be many causes for one symptom. Treating diseases is very important. Suppressing symptoms, however, is a little like telling the body to shut up. The danger is that we miss the underlying problem. Thinking of ADHD as a genetic disease gives the impression that there is a drug that will cure the problem when, in fact, it is simply suppressing the symptom. This may be fueling the epidemic use of stimulant medications. While medication may seem like a quick fix, it offers no long-term solution to the problem.

Quick Fixes

Treating symptoms can be a tricky business. For instance, treating your child's fever can sometimes make him feel more comfortable. But what if I were to tell you to treat your child's fever with Tylenol every day for the rest of his life? Any parent knows this simply doesn't sound right. But that's exactly what parents are often told to do when their child is diagnosed with ADHD and given a prescription. "Just keep him on it for the rest of his life. That should fix the problem."

For some children this can be a very dangerous practice. When we suppress symptoms, we miss the opportunity of understanding *why* a child is struggling. While this may ease suffering in the short term, it can be bad medicine in the long run. Suppose three kids come to me with a fever of 103 degrees. If I simply treat the symptom, I might get lucky with one child who simply had a cold and the next day is feeling better. But the parents of the second child might return saying, "Hey Doc, every time the Tylenol wears off, the fever comes back." Then I have to run more tests to look for underlying causes of the fever. Meanwhile, the third child may have died because he had some terrible disease like meningitis. Each child had the same symptom, a temperature of 103. But they had very different reasons for developing that symptom.

The same is true for children with the symptoms of ADHD. It's tempting to go for the quick fix when you see your child suffering. This may, in part, be fueled by the widespread availability of drugs like Ritalin. If there is a medicine that will take care of the symptom, why not use it right now? But by failing to look at the causes, what we may have here is not an epidemic of disease sweeping through our children but simply a boom in sales for the pharmaceutical industry.

Child Development Is Not a Race

Parents are put under enormous pressure to treat their child's ADHD quickly. This comes in part from the pressure teachers themselves are under to meet the increasingly narrow standards created by their curriculum. Their performance is being judged by how well their class is meeting these standards, and this leaves little room for considering the unique circumstances in a particular child's life. To be fair, no teacher or parent wants to see a child fall behind. Doctors also feel the pressure to fix the problem quickly. This kind of emergency thinking is fueling the need for quick fixes. But child development is not a race. Believe it or not, the fastest is not always the smartest. Each child has a unique stream of development.

To be clear, there *is* a place for medications in the treatment of ADHD. In any emergency, suppressing symptoms are helpful in temporarily reducing suffering. In situations where the context of a child's life is so chaotic and his self-esteem has dropped so low that he is in real danger, I have found that ADHD medications can be a "bridge" that buys a family time to make the kind of changes necessary to help a child develop attention. All too often, however, once a child is placed on medications, the underlying causes are simply ignored. This commits a child to a lifetime of medication.

A Culture of Speed

As a doctor treating children with ADHD, I found myself frustrated by a system that seems to leave the child out of the equation. When we ignore the particulars of a child's life and reduce him to chemistry, it's no surprise that the treatment is basically the same for all kids: chemical speed. Parents find it strange to put a hyperactive child on a stimulant medication (see list—common stimulants), but in a culture of speed, your child needs to hurry up and pay attention, to "get up to speed." While the exact mechanism of action of stimulant medications is not known, they appear to work by creating a chemical emergency in areas of the brain involved with vigilance (primarily dopamine and norepinephrine receptors) (Kim et al. 2009). They get these emergency centers fired up to focus as if it's a matter of life and death.

Common Stimulant Medications Available in the United States

Ritalin, Ritalin LA, Adderall, Adderall XR, Concerta, Daytrana TD, Dexadrine, Focalin, Focalin XR, Intuniv, Metadate, Methylin, Methylphenidate, Methylphenidate ER, Ritalin, Ritalin SR, Ritalin LA, Vyvance

---

Chemical Emergencies

As years went by, I became increasingly concerned about the long-term effects of placing children into states of "chemical emergency" during such vulnerable periods of their development. There is surprisingly little research available on the long-term safety and efficacy of these drugs in children. And there is certainly no evidence that these medications will cure the problem. What's more, children naturally adapt to the medication, so doses need to be constantly raised in order to keep their kick. And as the dose goes up, so do the side effects (see chart of adverse effects). Eventually, after exhausting all the choices of quick fixes, we find ourselves right back where we started.

Adverse Effects of Stimulant Medications

Nervousness and insomnia

Weight loss

Hypersensitivities (hives, fever, joint pain)

Exfoliative dermatitis (peeling skin)

Erythema multiforme (chronic rash)

Appetite suppression

Nausea; dizziness

Palpitations (irregular, hard, or rapid heartbeat)

Headache

Dyskinesia (muscle spasms)

Drowsiness

Blood pressure and pulse changes

Tachycardia (rapid heart rate)

Angina (caused by an insufficient supply of blood to the heart muscle)

Cardiac arrhythmia (irregularity of the heartbeat)

Abdominal pain

Tourette syndrome (tic disorders)

Drug-induced psychosis

(*Physician's Desk Reference* 2010)

Dissatisfied with this approach, I began to search for a better way to customize treatment. I wanted an approach that honors the unique way each child grows and learns. And I would begin to find it by looking at what actually influences a child's attention.

Chapter 2

Stress and Attention

To the attentive eye, each moment of the year has its own beauty and in the same field it beholds, every hour, a picture which was never seen before and which shall never be seen again.

Ralph Waldo Emerson

Summers spent at the beach on Cape Cod offered my children hours of amusement. When the tide went out, there were miles of sand stretching out to the horizon, a veritable laboratory of exploration in the puddles left behind. My kids and I would spend hours playing in this natural sandbox, transfixed by all the life revealed in those little worlds. Limitless adventures awaited them every morning when they awoke. Catching hermit crabs, the kids would create tiny habitats for them in plastic tubs back at the house. They would name them, take turns feeding them, and study the mysteries of their nature. This was sheer delight. Long after the sun had gone down, we would call the kids to come in, but they could barely hear us; such was their utter focus.

Basic Sanity

Spend some time living by the ocean or camping in the woods. You will find that within a few days or even hours your attention begins to "unwind." Something happens when you watch the sunrise and sunset every day or notice the stars coming out one by one at night. You begin to focus in a more relaxed way. You return to a kind of basic sanity in which your natural mental abilities can function effectively. We are, after all, nothing but nature, and studies have shown that the human nervous system functions at its peak when our heart rate and breathing patterns are synchronized to the natural rhythms of the world (McCraty and Childre 2010). Simply stated, we function best when we are less stressed. Just going to sleep when the sun goes down and waking when the sun comes up brings greater balance between our sympathetic (fight or flight) and parasympathetic (rest and digest) nervous systems. This permits us to adapt more effectively to the ever-changing circumstances of our lives. Research has shown that when children learn to pay attention to internal rhythms like hunger and sleep cycles, this too can improve their performance in daily activities (Johnson 2000).

Attention is linked to stress in many ways. Children growing up in our fast-paced modern world can get cut off from these natural rhythms. They spend long hours in front of a screen or sitting in a classroom. They eat when they're not hungry. They go to sleep long after they're tired and wake before they're ready to. These all contribute to an inability to regulate attention (Swing et al. 2010). The ability to regulate attention is linked to the stability of our emotional states. Important recent research tracking children for thirty years (from early childhood onward) has shown that the ability to regulate one's emotions (*self-regulation*) is just as predictive as socioeconomic status or IQ in determining a child's long-term academic, social, and economic success and physical well-being (Moffitt et al. 2011).

The Epigenetics of Attention

Our ability to regulate attention is directly linked to the nature of our circumstances. The World Health Organization recently emphasized the primary importance of the socio-environmental context as equal to one's physical condition in determining how well a child will function (Kraus de Camargo 2010). We do not live independently of our environment. The emerging field of *epigenetics* (the study of the effect of environmental changes on gene expression) has demonstrated just how adaptive our genes actually are. Genes switch on and off in a constant dialogue with the environment. This is what gives us our amazing diversity as a species and explains why two children with similar symptoms of ADHD may have very different causes and very different solutions to their problems.

Stress: Why Less Is More

To understand your child's attention problems holistically, my first step is always to look carefully at the context of her life. This doesn't mean looking to blame someone or something for your child's problems. It simply means carefully examining the balance of factors that are either supporting or undermining your child's sense of security. When a child feels insecure, she is not being supported in a way that nourishes her developmental needs. This naturally leads to an increase in stress.

Not all stress is bad. In fact, it may be critical for attention. Too little stress, and there's no motivation to learn—so you tune out. Too much stress causes overreactions that make it impossible to calmly pay attention. And so you tune out.

Optimum Stress

Hans Selye, sometimes called the "father of stress research," demonstrated over fifty years ago that stress plays a key role in growth and function (Selye 1978). Somewhere between the two extremes of too little and too much, there is an *optimum stress* that allows your child to focus clearly. Recent research has shown that optimum stress levels are much lower than one might expect. Ed Calabrese at the University of Massachusetts has been investigating the power of "low-dose stimulation" (*hormesis*) in such diverse fields as psychology, neurology, and toxicology (Mattson and Calabrese 2010). Nature seems to support growth according to the principle of "less is more." Laozi, an ancient Chinese philosopher, recommended "less is more" as the most effective way for dealing with life's challenges. This strategy is a radically different way of thinking about helping your child pay attention. Too often we tend to think that if some is good, more is better; that all it takes to make a child pay attention better is to push her harder or give her more. This is often rooted in our own urgency to fix things quickly. But I find that "more" simply doesn't work. If anything, it increases stress, making it harder to focus. What seems to work better is when we use our love as a guide in shaping a child's environment. We don't need to make big changes; we just need to be consistent and practice every day. The ancients described this kind of practice as similar to the way a small creek becomes a stream and eventually a river. You can make small changes to gradually improve your child's sense of security, allowing a new habit of attention to emerge. I call this the power of "less is love," and it begins by looking at all the forces at play in your child's life.

The Big Picture: What's Tuning Your Child?

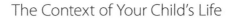

The Context of Your Child's Life

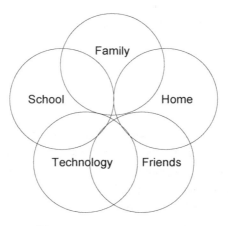

Children focus on what makes them feel secure and avoid what threatens their sense of security. We can map out five overlapping fields of security in your child's life and use them to shape the kind of optimum stress that will promote clearer attention.

The Family Womb

Family acts like a kind of second womb that nourishes your child's mind. This is where a sense of security begins. Our children model our behaviors from the moment they are born. Humans possess "mirror neurons" that help us mentally practice doing what others are doing. This is how we learn. What you pay attention to will naturally affect what your child pays attention to.

A family can also be a source of instability that hinders a child's ability to learn. Susan Anderson and Martin Teicher at Harvard University are among a number of researchers who have looked at the ways family stress actually alters the connections in a child's brain (Anderson and Teicher 2009). They have found that there are windows of time during childhood when the child is vulnerable to such things as prolonged maternal separation or marital dysfunction, and these can have long-lasting effects on the way a child's nervous system shapes itself. These stressors have been shown to contribute to many learning problems, including ADHD. I am not saying that your child's attention problem is your fault—that would be much too simple. I *am* saying that you are an important part of the solution.

Home: A Secure Base

A home is a nest. The actual structure of your home offers many opportunities to stimulate or hinder your child's attention. Mary Ainsworth, a pioneer in the field of child psychology attachment theory, has described the need for a secure base or "safe haven." This is where a child can return in order to release the tensions that come from exploring the outside world (Ainsworth et al. 1978). Having a safe haven has a profound effect on the way a child learns. We know from studies looking at children living in poverty that environmental deprivation causes serious developmental delays in children (Parker, Greer, and Zuckerman 1988). But a home can also be too stimulating. A child who has been overindulged may find it difficult to calmly focus.

Your child's home is the place where she learns to test the boundaries. An environment that is either too strict (not enough freedom to explore) or too loose (not enough boundaries to learn from) can threaten the delicate balance of optimum stress necessary to promote healthy attention.

I have found that even small changes in your child's room can actually reduce her stress level and allow her to focus more freely. The Chinese practice of *feng shui* ("healing the house") is an ancient tradition that recognizes the profound influences a home has on one's health and performance. Creating a calm environment and even simply changing the position of your child's bed or the color of her room can affect a child's attention (see resources).

Comfort Food

Eating is the most primal way we learn about the world. It's how we take in information, digest it, and make it a part of us. By information, I mean that which is conveyed through taste, texture, color, and temperature, as well as the actual nutrients we absorb. This process is directly related to how we pay attention. I often explore a child's attitudes about eating because it will give me clues about the way she is engaging with her world. Is she open to new experiences or rigid in her food choices? But it's not just *what* your child eats but *how much* she eats, *where* she eats, and *when* she eats that will determine the kind of optimum stress necessary for healthy attention.

WHAT WE EAT

Think of how careful you were when you first started feeding your baby. It was like a big experiment. Every parent knows that the quality of food affects the way a child grows. But something happens once a kid goes out into the world. Studies have shown that a diet consisting of fast food affects brain function. It can lead to a loss of specific nutrients important for brain growth and alter hormones secreted in the gut that affect neural connections important for attention (Gómez-Pinilla 2008). Foods grown organically produce higher amounts of phytochemicals (produced in plants) that work at the level of our genes to promote optimal brain function (Mattson 2008). This is an example of the principle of less is more. Fewer food additives equals more brain power. What we eat is important in treating ADHD, but I try to avoid making general recommendations because one size does not fit all. I will discuss specific dietary changes for specific types of ADHD later in this book.

WHERE WE EAT

In ancient times, eating was an important part of daily life. It brought people together as a clan. Eating together strengthens our bonds, reduces stress, and offers a secure place to exchange ideas and discuss the day's events. When your child eats in front of the TV or computer, it is amazing how quickly she will learn to tune out everything around her. Many children become too distracted to know when they're full. Advertisers take advantage of the hypnotic effects of TV to sell their products. It is estimated that food and beverage companies spend over $20 billion a year on television advertising to children. Simply reducing the time spent eating in front of the TV in favor of eating together is a simple way to improve your child's attention.

WHEN WE EAT

Timing is everything when it comes to eating. Our biological clock is designed to signal when it's time to eat. This keeps us connected to daily rhythms and seasonal cycles. Studies have shown that our sleep-wake cycle is linked to the hormones that affect hunger, attention, and memory (Taheri et al. 2004). People who don't get enough sleep crave more high-energy foods (like carbohydrates) that stoke the stress responses in our nervous system. Many children aren't ready to eat when they wake up if they haven't had enough sleep the night before. This is especially true for teenagers. These days, there's just not enough time in the morning to eat breakfast. Yet studies have shown how important breakfast is for improving school performance (Sibley et al. 2008). This is another simple way to improve your child's attention.

Some children seem to lose focus at specific times of the day. This can be a clue to the dietary influences. Children who load up on carbohydrates can develop *reactive hypoglycemia*, in which their blood sugar drops a few hours after eating. This dip makes it hard for them to focus on anything but getting more sugar. Developing strategies that meet the specific digestive needs of your child's metabolism can be a simple way to make big changes in his attention.

HOW MUCH WE EAT

I have found that simply getting your child to pay attention to when she's full or hungry is a very direct way to improve her attention. The hormone leptin tells us when we're full. It also stimulates brain connections. When we no longer pay attention to when we're full, we can become insensitive to the cognitive benefits of leptin too. There is a link between ADHD and the epidemic rise in obesity in our culture (Lam and Yang 2007). In fact, eating less has been shown to create the kind of optimum stress that promotes healthy cognitive function (Mattson 2008). Once again, we see the power of "less is more."

The Security of Friends

We often forget the powerful role that friends play in shaping your child's attention. As your child grows, she will have a tribal need to find her niche in a peer group. Their interests become her interests. Friends can become a secure base for a child, offering support when she cannot find it at home. They can also be a source of insecurity for the child who is having trouble fitting in. Studies have shown that children with ADHD are often rejected by their peers (Hinshaw and Melnick 1995). Children are sometimes hesitant to discuss peer problems with their parents out of shame or embarrassment. Or kids may feel that their parents wouldn't understand. This is an important factor to be considered when discovering what is influencing your child's attention.

The Society of School

Outside of the home, school becomes the place where your child spends a major part of her time learning to pay attention. This is where children are often most stressed. Unfortunately, school has begun to resemble a kind of factory where the pressures of standardization and policies like No Child Left Behind have put teachers in a terrible bind. Under enormous pressure to "teach to the test," there is little time to honor individual learning styles. Breaking this vicious cycle can be daunting for parents. Developing solutions for your child's attention problems requires a good working relationship between you and her teachers. The more consistent the plan between home and school, the faster your child will develop new habits of attention. I will discuss specific recommendations for teachers when we look at the different types of ADHD.

The Web of Technology

The digital revolution has brought us an ever-growing array of sophisticated and attractive things to pay attention to. From the moment our children are born they are bathed in a world of high-speed visual stimuli. I see one-year-olds sitting on their mothers' laps, intensely figuring out games on their mother's cell phones as they wait for me to examine them. Children have been referred to as "digital natives," while adults remain "digital immigrants," those who can speak the language but not fluently. We take pride in their amazing skill at multitasking. But there is mounting evidence that the increasing demands of multitasking come with a cost on how well we learn. *Cognitive flexibility* is a term used to describe the way we shift from one focus to the next. This is critically important for good attention. Recent studies at Stanford have shown that the mind does not really multitask at all (Ophir, Nass, and Wagner 2009). It may look like that's what your child is doing when she's sitting in front of the TV while instant-messaging, eating dinner, and doing homework. But in reality, the mind is simply jumping very quickly from one activity to another, often at the expense of quality and efficiency. This multitasking behavior may actually be increasing stress. Studies done in such stressful places like air traffic control centers and emergency rooms have shown that multitasking actually leads to "interrupt-driven" errors that can have potentially fatal consequences (Rubinstein, Meyer, and Evans 2001).

Because technology is a reality in our lives, I spend a lot of time exploring its effects with families. Parents often tell me that while their child can't pay attention in school, she seems to have no problem spending hours glued to video games at home. In fact, some parents think video games actually help a child's attention and indeed, studies have confirmed that playing video games can improve spatial cognition (Spence and Feng 2010). But I find that, for some children, use of technology directly contributes to their problems in school.

THE SLOW-MODEM SYNDROME

Here's a little experiment you can try at home to see what it feels like to be your digital-native child. If you have a really fast connection to the Internet, try using an old dial-up 56k modem. Remember when you first had a modem like that? At the time, most of us were amazed at how fast it was. But now it feels like torture watching the screen slooowly download an image. Most of you won't even dare try this. What's the point? It's simply too frustrating, too boring, and too slow. That's exactly what it feels like when your child has adapted to video technology at home and now is forced to pay attention to a teacher talking in school. Where are all the cool visuals? Where are the 200-point rewards every few seconds, reinforcing attention? The brain can't help but adapt to faster, more efficient ways of doing things, and going backward simply feels frustrating and boring.

We can't blame our children for adapting to their environment. They're simply surviving. It's the classroom that seems to be moving in slow motion, and that may be why kids seem to need speed to make it more exciting.

The Five Powers of Attention

Digital technology has shed light on how we focus. John Charlton was one of the first researchers to look at gaming addiction ("gaming" referring to video games). Charlton classified qualities of attention that I have adapted in understanding the different ways children use and lose focus (Charlton and Danforth 2007). I call these the *the five powers of attention*, and they will be important later in this book.

- *Immersion* refers to the ability to be so deeply involved with the game that one loses track of time, literally disassociating from the real world.

- *Flow* is the feeling of "being in the zone" when the challenge is set just slightly beyond one's skill.

- *High engagement* is the feeling of exhilaration that comes from being rewarded each time you get points. This "high" is what makes the game so addicting.

- *Presence* is the sense of reality we get from playing the game, the feeling of actually being right there in the game, as if it were real.

- *Precision* refers to the state of cognitive absorption that comes from figuring out the logic of the game. This state helps us develop strategies to win.

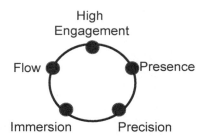

It's not hard to imagine how valuable these powers were for our ancestors when they were hunting in the forest. Immersion, flow, high engagement, presence, and precision are exactly the qualities we wish our children would have while they're sitting in the classroom or doing homework. If they have such powers to tune in while watching TV or playing video games, why can't they do it in school? In order to answer that, we have to look more closely at which part of the brain is dominating your child's attention.

Chapter 3

Taking a Closer Look: The Three Treasures

A tense mind will not be able to focus on anything for long.

Chan Master Sheng Yen

Max was ten years old when he first came to see me. He was being sent to yet another school. He had been asked to leave his last school because his teachers said that he was disruptive in the classroom. He would blurt out comments like "This is boring" if he didn't like something. Sometimes he'd throw tantrums that seemed to come out of nowhere. This volatility scared the teachers and other kids. He had seen several doctors and had tried a series of medications for ADHD, but each drug worked for only a few weeks before losing its effectiveness. When we met, he was having difficulty sleeping and was living on a diet consisting mainly of bread and soda. He was restless and impatient with my questions, barking short responses. He finally yelled, "This is a waste of time!" and bolted out of my office, leaving his teary-eyed mother and me staring at each other. That was twelve years ago. He eventually came back to work with me and is now in his second year of college. It looks like he's on track to become a successful lawyer.

Living in the world is a great adventure. It takes brains to survive in such an ever-changing environment. We humans are truly gifted. In fact, we have three brains, not just one, to play with. When I tell parents this they look at me like I have three heads. And in a way, I do!

Dr. Paul MacLean first described the theory of the three brains (what he called "The Triune Brain Model") back in the 1960s while at the National Institutes of Health researching the neurological basis of emotions (1973). What he discovered was that our neural structures mirror our evolution as a species from reptile to mammal to human. This remarkable discovery is extremely important in understanding why your child seems distracted. We are all wired to pay attention. But how we focus depends on which of these three treasures is dominating our lives.

Knowing by Heart

One of my first delights in studying Chinese medicine came when I discovered that the same word is used to define mind and heart: *xin*. I find this amazing. In English, we say we feel things with our hearts but use our brains to figure things out. But we can *know* things by heart and our brain can *feel* confused. However, something wonderful happens when I use "heart" instead of "mind" in working with children. Suddenly love enters the field of neurology.

The Little Frog Heart

Imagine a frog sitting in his swampy home. A fly buzzes by and *snap!* The frog catches it without batting an eye. Next try holding your breath. Eventually something takes over and makes you exhale. You can't help it. Deep in each human brain stem there lies a treasure that allows us to pay attention to the basic rhythms that keep us alive. Your heart beats, you breathe in and out, you get sleepy and need to take a nap, you get hungry and need to eat. The "reptile brain," or "R-complex," as MacLean called it, keeps a close eye on these basic functions. This attention is how we stay connected to the source of the natural cycles of life. I call this the *little frog heart*. Like the frog waiting for the fly then snapping, somewhere in the background of our consciousness, we humans keep the rhythm of our day-to-day life regulated in order to maintain homeostatic balance. When we try to voluntarily control our breath, we see just how powerful this little frog heart is. Focused on the basic circadian rhythms of sleeping, eating, breathing, and pooping, its primitive power can override our voluntary will in order to keep us alive and connected to our environment.

Some children with ADHD show signs that their little frog heart is in trouble. They may have trouble falling asleep or they may sleep too much. They may be unable to eat or they may eat too much. They may hyperventilate or they may hold their breath. They may get constipated or they may have diarrhea. These can be serious signs that the stress in a child's life has overwhelmed even the most basic reflexes of attention.

The Wild Puppy Heart

Now think of a puppy barking in the front yard at the mailcarrier: "Emergency! Emergency! Intruder alert! Mailman! Mailman!" Puppies have the kind of energy and immediacy that characterize the second of our three brains.

Sitting just above the frog brain, we find what MacLean called the "limbic system." This is responsible for many of the powerful emotional responses to the world that are so important to our survival. Unlike the little frog heart, the limbic system drives our intense desires and aversions. It is this treasure that holds our emotional memories, urging us to search for security when we feel threatened. I call this the *puppy heart* because of the intense feelings we have in the moment. Many parents laugh at this analogy because their kids do sometimes act just like puppies. That's what makes them so cute and sometimes so wild. When conditions are not optimal, when your child feels too insecure, he's bound to express it in dramatic ways. In those moments, it's difficult for him to think about anyone else. All we hear is the barking of "Me first!" that can transform his true powers of attention into exaggerated symptoms of ADHD.

Now let's look at some of the ways that puppy heart can shift a child's powers of attention.

FROM HIGH ENGAGEMENT TO IMPULSIVITY

"I want it! I want it! I want it *now!*" Sometimes a child will get so excited by something that he simply can't wait another second. He is focused on the sheer pleasures of life. Much of child's play is filled with this wonderful joy. It's what makes the power of high engagement so much fun. He literally gets high on life. But when conditions are too stimulating, some children can no longer control these impulses. That's when the puppy heart starts barking.

A puppy lives in "the now." "Oh boy, oh boy! We're going for a walk!" and the puppy ends up peeing on the floor. This loss of control is a sign that the puppy heart has gotten too wild and is overriding what the little frog heart is focused on. In the classroom, a child may blurt out the answer because he's so excited. Some children are so sensitive that they have complete meltdowns when they're overstimulated. Others who have become addicted to high levels of stimulation may find it difficult to pay attention to anything that doesn't offer the thrill of novelty. That's when we hear children complaining that they're bored all the time. This dependency on stimulation can create a vicious cycle—the more bored, the more distracted by the slightest thing. And when this dynamic becomes a habit, it's very difficult to learn anything.

FROM FLOW TO HOSTILITY

"Hey, that's my toy; don't touch it!" When we feel secure, we can rise up and explore challenges by going with the flow. To the puppy heart, it feels like we're "in the zone." But when things are too challenging, they threaten our confidence and frustrations turn into outbursts of anger. Some children may lash out as if out of nowhere. Like a dog snarling if you get too near his bone, the puppy heart can go into high alert: senses heighten, making things appear even more threatening than they may be. Children get caught in a vicious cycle here because there is no tolerance for this kind of "barking" in a classroom. In reality, it is just the puppy heart trying to let us know it's a threatening situation. To the teacher, the child is hyperactive or, worse, hostile. I see this behavior as a cry for help, but because it is so volatile and unpredictable in a child, it can send worried parents to doctors for prescriptions.

FROM PRECISION TO RIGIDITY

"I can't start that until I finish this!" We are all creatures of habit. Winter or summer, my dog will take the same route from the house into the woods to do her business, wearing away a permanent path in my lawn. Routine gives us a sense of security that allows us to predict what's going to happen next. The puppy heart focuses on patterns to make sense out of the world. But when things don't go according to plan, when change happens too fast, feelings get amplified, turning the power of precision into a rigid state of hyperfocusing. We get stuck in an effort to prevent too much change. For some children, this kind of inflexibility can turn into compulsion. Some children with ADHD are not distractible, but instead have trouble shifting their focus. Getting stuck on details, they can't see the forest for the trees. This, too, is a cry for help. Transitions seem more threatening than they are. The need for rigidity in the face of inconsistency impedes the natural flexibility needed to pay attention in the classroom.

FROM IMMERSION TO WITHDRAWAL

"I won't do that! You can't make me!" Our ability to retreat from danger is as much a treasure of the puppy heart as is our ability to fight to survive. When a dog hears thunder, it hides under the bed and won't be budged. Some children can get so caught up in things they're doing that they have no idea what's happening around them. When they are overstressed or frightened, they may appear to shut down by escaping into their own world. This is when the power of immersion turns into withdrawal. Some children may use this coping mechanism when they feel insecure, withdrawing from all interactions with others. Some children with ADHD will stubbornly refuse to participate in the classroom. Others get lost in their own daydreams. For some, it's impossible to get them motivated to do their schoolwork. And the more you push them, the more threatened they feel and the more they withdraw. This kind of puppy barking may not be explosive, but it's just as disruptive to learning. When it becomes a habit it can lead to apathy and even paranoia, which is extremely worrisome for parents and teachers.

FROM PRESENCE TO WORRY

"If you do it, I'll do it." We humans are social beings and can't help but pay attention to what others are doing. We find security in the bonds we make with others. MacLean suggested that the "separation call"—like when puppies bark when separated from the pack—may be the most important evolutionary development that distinguishes mammals from reptiles (1985). Calling out when we're separated is linked to family bonding, language, and even play skills. It's how we stay connected. When separation is too sudden or too prolonged, the puppy heart amplifies feelings of insecurity and anxiety that make it impossible to focus on anything besides finding that contact. That's when a child loses his sense of being present. Some children with ADHD have underlying attachment problems (Marazziti et al. 2008). Their worry makes it impossible for them to learn anything in a classroom.

A HOUSE ON FIRE

To be clear, the puppy heart is not bad. It's what makes life so rich and exciting. These amplified perceptions and expressions allow us to understand the world through our feelings. This is key to surviving. When your house is on fire, you have to get out. But when the puppy dominates the scene even when there's no fire, you are no longer in sync with what's happening. That's when amplified perceptions insist on "me first," making it extremely difficult to calmly pay attention, listen, and learn from someone else. If you have a child with ADHD, you may recognize these puppy-heart expressions. Remember, this kind of barking is a natural cry for help. It reflects your child's level of insecurity. It can also feed the vicious cycle of low self-esteem, but it doesn't mean she has a disease. It's just her puppy barking. We're not just frogs or dogs, however. There's another treasure we all possess that is concerned with much more than just putting "me first."

The Big Heart

Out of the limbic system, we have evolved the *neocortex*, literally "the new brain," which makes up the bulk of our neural matter. This is what shapes much of our individuality as we grow up. It allows us to connect the dots in broader ways, to tie past memories to experiences of a wider range of emotions without getting locked into narrow reaction patterns. It is this newer brain that gives us the freedom to step back and see the world in new ways. The neocortex is the treasure that holds our creativity. By connecting to the limbic system it can regulate our puppy-heart impulses, allowing us to take a step back from our immediate danger and see the "big picture." By doing so, we can think about the needs of others, not just "me first." This is how we develop tolerance for the diversity of others. By seeing others express their experiences, we're able to share ideas more creatively. The neocortex gives us the power to express a broader range of emotional states with greater subtlety and depth, giving us a better chance of being understood by others. I call this treasure *the big heart* and can sum up all its qualities with one word: imagination.

Close your eyes and imagine for a moment that you're at the beach. Instantly you may see the golden sand, see the sun in the blue sky, and even hear the sound of the waves. And then, in the next instant, you're right back here, reading this. What a miracle! Carl Sagan said, "Imagination will often carry us to worlds that never were. But without it we go nowhere" (Sagan 1985, 4). No other animal has this power to travel to another place in their mind.

But imagination is not just a sightseeing excursion. It's also the great source of our ingenuity as a species. We humans have the power to imagine what someone else is thinking or feeling and identify with that person's experience as if that thought or those feelings were our own. This is the root of compassion. We can imagine the consequences of our actions and make plans for the future. This is the root of our courage to make decisions. We have the power to imagine creative ways of expressing our feelings through metaphor and analogy. This is the root of poetry and storytelling. We can imagine the hidden reasons for why things happen, to connect the dots in elaborate ways that make sense out of the world. This is the root of our ethical behavior and reason. We can imagine seeing ourselves in context, to imagine new solutions for old problems, to discover the deeper meanings in life. This is the root of our self-reflection and self-consciousness.

Psychologists call these abilities our *executive functions*. Like executives working on the top floor, they are able to see where the business needs to go in order to be most successful. They are able to perceive the big picture and coordinate a plan of action. The neocortex of a child is shaped over time by his experiences. Children are not born with sophisticated executive functions. This lies at the heart of a developmental perspective and is the reason why it's inappropriate to expect a three- or four-year-old to be able to pay attention like an older child. If circumstances support a child's nature as he matures, he learns how to regulate his body, expand his emotional experiences, and express himself in ways that deepen his self-awareness. Through self-reflection he can see himself within the larger context of his life and is able to consider the effect he is having on others. As a child develops his big heart, he brings balance to the wild puppy-heart impulses and, in so doing, is able to focus calmly in stressful situations. Indeed, studies have shown that ADHD is a delay in the maturation process of the neocortex rather than an absence of some neurologic structure or chemical (Shaw et al. 2007). This means that attention can be developed in any child. It just takes time and practice.

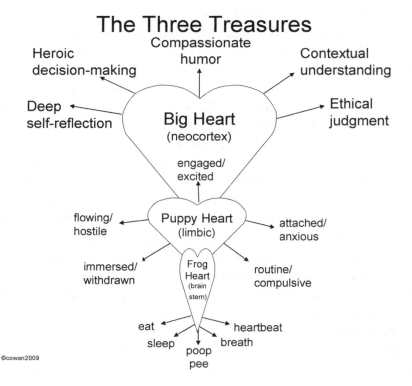

The Three Treasures

Big Sam

The powers of the big heart became very personal for me back in the 1980s when I was an idealistic young pediatric intern working in one of the hospitals in New York City. I found myself in the midst of horrific things: children abused, gunshot wounds, death, and suffering. My first instinct was to run away and cry. I had to learn how to stay calm and focused in order to help my patients. I was lucky; I had a wonderful role model.

One late night working in the ER, I saw two small children brought in, each in the midst of a life-threatening asthma attack. One child was being treated by a doctor who was barking orders at the nurses, who were running hysterically in and out of the room. The other was being treated by a doctor known as "Big Sam." Sam was an imposing, 300-pound physician who spoke with the softest, gentlest voice and had a way of putting everyone at ease whenever he entered a room. What I saw that night would change my life forever. In the first room, where there had been so much commotion, mistakes had been made and the additional stress the child was exposed to from the doctor had exacerbated her respiratory distress. She died. On the other hand, Big Sam's patient seemed to miraculously get better and didn't even require hospital admission. Sam's big heart had allowed him to stay focused on the big picture in a stressful situation, and this had had a remarkable effect on everyone around him. It was Big Sam who taught me how to develop my own big heart and use it during those grueling years of training ahead.

Three Hearts Are Better Than One

The more we practice developing our big-heartedness, the more secure our wild puppy heart becomes and the more intimate our little frog heart can be with the natural rhythms of the world. This is the key to understanding how to help any child suffering from the symptoms of ADHD. But in order for your child to become a true master of attention, we have to take a closer look at exactly who *your* child is and what type of ADHD symptoms he has.

Chapter 4

The Five Ways of Focus

To everything there is a season, and a time for
every purpose under heaven...

Ecclesiastes 3:1–8

Nature favors diversity. Changing circumstances elicit different responses, which in turn perpetuate change. Humans have diverse talents that enable them to survive in a range of conditions. If one way of adapting doesn't work, then someone else in the tribe may have a way that might. This has been the source of our amazing creativity, ingenuity, and power to dominate the planet.

Society favors conformity. In order to maintain order in big groups, we need to live by rules and regulations. This is how we function cohesively and meet common challenges that threaten our survival. It is the balance between our natural diversity and our need for conformity that determines our state of comfort and security.

Don't Throw the Baby Out with the Bathwater

Unfortunately, our need to conform has brought us increasingly artificially structured institutions (like school) that don't always address the diverse ways children learn. When a child's nature is ignored, this is bound to trigger exaggerated puppy-heart responses that intefere with calm attention. Conventional assessments of ADHD seem to follow this trend too, focusing on symptoms and leaving the individual qualities of the child out of the equation. Fifteen years ago, out of frustration with this assembly-line mentality, I set out to find another way of evaluating children that respected their unique nature. I would eventually find it in Chinese medicine. This ancient system of medicine had developed an ecological understanding of health problems as a reflection of the interplay of one's temperament in the context of the forces of nature. Over the years I have adapted this system to create a new perspective on child development and have found it to be a wonderful way of helping thousands of children overcome their symptoms of ADHD.

Not all children lose focus in exactly the same way. The qualities of each child's attention are linked to her particular adaptive style, or temperament. Many years ago, my dear friends and teachers Harriet Beinfield and Efrem Korngold opened my eyes to a deeper way of understanding temperament through their book *Between Heaven and Earth* (1992). In it they described "The Five Phase Correspondences" that link our emotional tendencies to our physical form. Together these will determine the unique way we respond to the world in which we live. This holistic perspective stands in stark contrast to Western psychological models of temperament that make little attempt at connecting the mind and body.

The Five Ways of the Heart

We each move through the world in distinct ways. The language of Chinese medicine is rooted in metaphors of the seasons: spring, summer, harvest, autumn, and winter. Each has distinct qualities and movements that reflect five forces of nature: Wood, Fire, Earth, Metal, and Water. Wood pushes out, Fire lights up, Earth integrates, Metal cuts apart, and Water goes deep. These qualities define our physical and mental tendencies and are an essential aspect of our basic sanity—that is, the way we connect to the natural cycles and rhythms of life (see Five Phase diagram).

Here we arrive at the heart of this book. This language may at first seem strange to you, but in it you will discover a new way of describing your child in more natural terms that avoid the impersonal pathological labels that burden conventional Western medicine. Rather than simply looking at what's wrong with your child, we can begin to map out a way to help your child develop her attention so that her treasures can truly shine.

Each season has a particular attraction. If you have a child who is distracted, I find that the best place to start is by asking what she is attracted to. Attractions become distractions only when a child's puppy heart is dominating her attention. As you read the following sections, consider what kind of force of nature your child most resembles. Please remember that we each possess some aspects of all five seasons, depending on the circumstances and which developmental stage we're passing through, but I find that there is usually a predominant theme that rings true for every child. This will be important in customizing your approach to helping your child. Parents' own natures often color their perspective on their child's nature. This often reveals important information about family relationships and is why I typically request both parents to be present if possible at the initial evaluation of a child. Since you are a vital part of your child's environment, consider which of the five natures you possess while reading this chapter. This will help you discover how to be part of the solution by cultivating qualities in yourself that will help your child pay attention more effectively.

Basic Sanity of the Five Phases

Summer
(fire)

Spring
(wood)

Harvest
(earth)

Winter
(water)

Autumn
(metal)

The Wood Child

Wood corresponds to the season of spring, when life bursts out of the dead of winter with incredible power. Nothing can hold back the spring. Plants push through the ground. Even tiny blades of grass push through cracks in the sidewalk. Green leaves burst through the thick bark overnight. Vines scramble across the ground and climb up walls. Everything is in motion. Birds clamor as they urgently build their nests. We cannot help but feel the force of nature in spring. According to Five Phase Correspondences, spring's power is captured in the movement of wood pushing through the ground. Its sound is the wind gusting in the trees. Green is its color. The green light of spring says, "Go!" We find it in the movements of our muscles, tendons, and nerves. It opens in our eyes each morning at sunrise when we rise and stretch to meet the challenges of the day.

The Wood Child Tuned In

The Wood child reflects all this springtime energy. She wakes early and is ready to go. Even before they can walk, Wood children have a fascination with the way things move and are eager to explore their world by pushing boundaries. We say they are "kinesthetic learners" and "sensory seekers," needing to touch things and manipulate them in order to understand them. Tuned in to the world, the treasure of their big heart shines. They become our true heroes. When they are "in the zone," their power of attention flows as they rise to meet challenges with courage and flexibility.

The archetype of the Wood child is the pioneer, the explorer. Curiosity motivates him to keep moving forward, breaking new boundaries. Thomas Edison had a classic Wood sensibility. His independent mind got him kicked out of school at an early age, but we'd be sitting in the dark without his inventiveness.

Wood children crave the thrill of adventure, sometimes without any sense of fear (much to the dismay of parents). This is perhaps why they tend to love video games so much—the faster and more violent the better.

Physically, Wood children tend to be lean and muscular and their flexibility and coordination make them natural athletes. In ancient times, they played a key role in the tribe as scouts and skilled hunters.

Wood children are intensely proud. They are driven to be first, to win, and they hate losing. As adults, it's this boldness that makes them successful entrepreneurs. America is a Wood culture. Our heroes are the pioneers who settled this land. We honor our trailblazers, the rugged individualists whose love of freedom made the United States so rich and powerful. While we cherish these qualities in our adults, they can be daunting for any parent or teacher who has to contend with a Wood child as she is growing up. It's no accident that Wood children are often the first to be referred for symptoms of ADHD.

Wood Attractions/Distractions

The Wood child is naturally attracted to and distracted by movement. Anything that moves inspires exploration. Consequently, when nothing is moving around her or, even worse, when the Wood child herself isn't allowed to move, she can feel that her nature is being ignored. You can see how sitting in a static classroom environment might threaten the Wood child's puppy heart and amplify every little movement into a distraction.

The Wood Child Tuned Out

When the Wood child's freedom to move is inhibited, the power of flow can turn into frustration, hyperactivity, and hostility. These are the signs that the puppy heart is barking. When the Wood child has been cut off from exploring her world through movement, she begins acting like a caged animal. She can no longer sit still or focus calmly. She may shout out, "That's not fair!" In fact, shouting is the classic expression of the Wood child's state of insecurity.

School is where the Wood child often feels these constraints most. The Wood child's idea of "circle time" in preschool is running *around* the circle. Often parents will hear that their child is too "hyper" and needs to be tested for ADHD.

These are signs that a Wood child is tuning out a world that is threatening. She begins craving strong sensory input, which can make her vulnerable to the intensity of something like video games. Often, these games aren't just fun for the Wood child—they become an addiction. The more she plays, the less she wants to be in school, setting up a vicious cycle by compounding her insecurity in the classroom. Showing no fear of authority figures, the Wood child finds herself punished by frustrated parents and teachers. Increasingly sensitive to criticism, her behaviors become more exaggerated and disruptive.

Anger is the primal expression of the Wood child's puppy heart. If pushing boundaries is how she learns, then push comes to shove when she's insecure. Over time it's common for these kids to develop tension headaches and muscle twitching, physical manifestations of their stress.

Sleep and the Wood Child

In a chronic state of insecurity, the puppy heart dominates the frog heart. Difficulty falling asleep and restless sleep are characteristic signs of an overstressed Wood child. Some Wood children will have prolonged problems with bed-wetting. So caught up in their dreams, they've lost the connection to their reflex to hold their urine at night. This can be humiliating and frustrating for both child and parent. Because Wood children tend to wake up so early, they often don't get adequate sleep. Over time, this further destabilizes their attention.

Because of her hyperactivity, it may be tempting to think that the Wood child has the classic symptoms of ADHD. But as we will see, there are children with very different characteristics who are also struggling to focus.

Characteristics of the Wood Child

Tuned In (Big Hearted)	Tuned Out (Puppy Hearted)	Physical Signs of Tuning Out
"The True Hero"	"The Wild Child"	Squirming, twitching
Attracted to movement, exploring	Distracted by stillness	Muscle spasms
The power of "flowing"	Doesn't "go with the flow"	Frequent headaches
Physically adept	Hyperactive, fidgety	Migrating nerve pain
Heroic love of exploring	Hates being restrained	Recurrent bed-wetting
Up to the challenge	Easily frustrated	Cravings: stimulants, sugars, soda, butter
Learns physically	Overconfident, doesn't want help	Fears: judgment, confinement, loss of pride, not winning
Goal driven, hates losing	Rushes through work	Cry: *"I'll do it my way!"*
Loves the thrill of danger	Ready to "pounce"	
Pushes boundaries	Argumentative	
Argues effectively	Explosive anger, easily provoked	
Archetype: The Pioneer	No respect for authority figures	

The Fire Child

Fire corresponds to the season of summer. In contrast to the push of spring, plants have now reached the culmination of their growth and have burst open in flowers displaying rich colors and fragrances, attracting the bees and butterflies. This is the time of great consummation, of pollination. It's party time! The weather is hotter, forcing us to slow down and take it easy. People go on vacation, distracting themselves with sightseeing. It's a time to have fun, to try something new. Fire brings light and excitement to all our celebrations. Think of the fireworks of the Fourth of July, the sky bursting with flower-like explosions of light. In summer, light fills the long days. In our daily cycle, Fire corresponds to the midday sun. Its color is red, the color of blood. The dramatic red light says stop and smell the roses. Physically we feel it when we blush, in our quickening heartbeat, in our circulation.

The Fire Child Tuned In

It's hard not to notice the Fire child's bright spirit, even when she's a baby. Like a summer flower, her spirit draws others in with her excitement. Tuned in, the treasure of her big heart shines, enabling her to become a true leader in the world. Her power of attention is a sense of high engagement with everything new in the world. Martin Luther King Jr. had the classic Fire temperament in his power to move mountains with his words.

Fire children are extremely intuitive, feeling things that the rest of us may miss. Like a single candle burning in the dark, the Fire child lights up the whole room with her charm, but even the slightest breeze can make her flicker. Such is the Fire child's extreme sensitivity to change.

Like the Wood child, the Fire child is outgoing, and sensory seeking, but rather than pushing boundaries, she absorbs stimulation. As she gets older, her happy-go-lucky nature makes her popular with everyone. The Fire child loves being silly and tries hard to get others to be silly too. She doesn't have the same edge that the Wood child has in challenging authority. Her charisma makes her a natural-born leader. Though she may not always be comfortable in the spotlight if it's not spontaneous, she can't help but be entertaining. The archetype of Fire is the wizard, who seems to spontaneously create magic wherever she goes. The Fire child craves intensity but is easily startled when things happen too fast or unexpectedly. That's when you hear the excessive barking of her puppy heart.

Fire Attractions/Distractions

The Fire child is attracted to the novelty of stimulation. Anything that feels new feels alive and thoroughly engages her. This attraction can become addictive, even if sudden change sometimes overwhelms her. This can set the stage for a particular kind of insecurity, when there's either too much stimulation or not enough. The Fire child can't tolerate feeling bored, and that's when the attraction to the littlest sensation becomes distracting, making it impossible to focus on anything for long.

The Fire Child Tuned Out

The Fire child is prone to dramatic swings in emotions. One minute she's laughing, the next she's crying. This can amplify her sense of insecurity, culminating in panic. There is nothing more intimidating to the Fire child than being told it's time to be serious. To tune this out, it's not uncommon to find her becoming the class clown in an attempt to lighten up the situation. Acting on the slightest whim, she may appear impulsive. This sets up a vicious cycle: feeling out of control, her senses become amplified, and she may jump when startled or complain that the tags on her shirts bother her. These are all signs of a cry for help—the puppy heart is dominating.

In the classroom, the Fire child (like the Wood child) may be hyperactive. But rather than challenging authority, she does the least amount of work in order to go have fun. Like a hummingbird in a summer garden, she's always looking for something to play with, jumping from one object to the next, forgetting about the teacher talking in the front of the room. I find this degree of impulsivity corresponds to the Fire child's level of insecurity. Acting without thinking is often followed by remorse, because ultimately the Fire child really just wants everyone to love her. But the harder she tries, the more outrageous she gets. Some Fire children hold it together in school only to have dramatic meltdowns as soon as they get home.

Physically, the Fire child's metabolism tends to burn too hot when she's out of control. This can cause blood-sugar instabilities that worsen the dramatic mood swings. Fire children tend to crave carbohydrates in an attempt to satisfy their intense hunger. They are prone to explosive diarrhea, sweating, flushing, hives, or reflux when they are in prolonged states of over-excitement. As small children, Fire children can get so caught up in the excitement of the moment that they forget to go to the bathroom. This is a sign that the puppy heart is overriding the little frog heart, causing chronic constipation and *encopresis,* a condition of stool leakage resulting from impaction.

Sleep and the Fire Child

The Fire child burns so brightly she will often collapse when it's time to sleep or become overly dramatic if she gets overtired. She may talk in her sleep and, like the Wood child, may be prone to bed-wetting. Without enough sleep, her behaviors become extreme, and getting adequate sleep may have a profound effect on her attention.

A WORD OF CAUTION: RISK-TAKING BEHAVIOR AND THE FIRE CHILD

The Fire child's attraction to intense feelings puts her at risk for addictive behaviors during adolescence. Unlike the Wood child, who may be drawn to drugs and alcohol because of the danger of breaking the rules, the Fire child is attracted to the euphoria of drugs as a way to tune out the pressures of the world as she gets older.

Characteristics of the Fire Child

Tuned In (Big Hearted)	Tuned Out (Puppy Hearted)	Physical Signs of Tuning Out
"The True Leader"	"The Class Clown"	Flushing
Attracted to anything new	Distracted by change	Excessive sweating
The power of high engagement	Easily addicted	Hypoglycemia
Charismatic, charming	Provocative	Dramatic symptoms come and go
Fun loving	Impulsive, unpredictable	Prone to explosive diarrhea, encopresis
Never bored	Hypersensitive	Prone to palpitations, reflux
Enthusiastic	Complains of being bored	Difficulty falling asleep
Intuitive	Easily startled, panicked	Cravings: sweets, spicy food, ice
Jumping, dancing, singing	Frenzied, over the top	Fears: the dark, not being loved
Loves drama, the entertainer	Rapidly changing moods	Cry: "*I can't help myself!*"
Archetype: The Wizard		

The Earth Child

Earth corresponds to the harvest season. Living in the modern, industrialized world, we often forget how important the harvest is. And yet this is that special moment of transition between the hot months and the cooler months when everything ripens. Harvest is the culmination of the hot summer's work, the time when flowers transform into fruit. Think of the care taken in choosing just the right day in the vineyard to pick the grapes. Too soon or too late and the harvest is ruined.

In ancient times, this "fifth season" was a time when families came together to harvest the crops and celebrate the fruits of their labors, giving thanks with a harvest festival. This is when we take stock of the year's events, hear stories of each other's lives, and make plans for the coming months. All that's left of this humble season in our modern culture is Thanksgiving, which originally took place during "Indian Summer."

Earth represents the center of our daily life, just as the harvest stands at the center of the seasons. Though we all depend on it, we sometimes take it for granted. The earth accepts our planting and our garbage. In the daily cycle, Earth corresponds to the afternoon. In Mediterranean cultures it still has meaning in the siesta, a time to pause in the midst of work. We feel Earth in our stomach when we pause to digest the world. Its color is the yellow light of hesitation.

The Earth Child Tuned In

The Earth child is sweet, like the ripening fruit. She likes to be in the middle of things and cares deeply about the social group. But the Earth child prefers to stay in the background, sometimes going unnoticed. Tuned in, the treasure of his big heart shines, enabling him to become a true caregiver in the world. His power of attention is being present and attending to people's needs. Thoughtful and trustworthy, the Earth child is genuinely concerned with maintaining attachments, whether with family or friends. Earth children want to please. The archetype of Earth is the peacemaker. She is naturally interested in the way things are related. Characters with Earth nature don't always become famous because they prefer to work in the background. Mother Teresa is an Earth role model. Earth characters are the trusty sidekicks in our stories.

Earth children learn through context. If information is presented out of context, it becomes impossible for the child to understand its significance or retain it. Earth children find a greater sense of security in contact with others. They love the give-and-take of conversations, and their attachment to family, friends, clubs, and teams defines their loyalty. They may not care whether their team wins or loses as long as everyone stays together. In fact, they might actually feel bad if the other side loses.

Physically, Earth children tend to be fleshy and round in shape and as infants are sometimes called "Buddha babies." They are often prone to digestive problems when insecure.

Earth Attractions/Distractions

Earth children are attracted to maintaining attachments. Consequently, separation becomes their great distraction. When secure, the Earth child focuses on organizing seemingly disparate aspects of the world into a coherent whole. When insecure, she can lose direction, becoming confused and indecisive. That's a sign that the puppy heart is barking and it's impossible to pay attention.

The Earth Child Tuned Out

The Earth child's insecurity is amplified by feeling disconnected. Unable to think about anything else, she expresses excessive worry. This response makes it impossible to concentrate. At home, the natural peacemaker worries when others aren't getting along. She often finds herself caught in the middle of arguments, unable to choose sides. To avoid upsetting her parents, she may hide her worries, inwardly blaming herself for others' problems. Prolonged separation anxiety may be the first sign of exaggerated insecurity.

In school, the Earth child prefers to work by committee. The more she's forced to work independently, the more difficult she finds it to pay attention, setting up a vicious cycle of obsessive anxieties.

While it may be hard not to notice the insecure Fire or Wood child, Earth children tend to fall through the cracks for many years. They may look like they are paying attention because they want to please the teacher, but they may have no idea what's going on if their learning style is being ignored. It's not until third or fourth grade, when the work pressures mount, that it becomes obvious they're overwhelmed. Often the first signs are vague physical complaints, particularly stomachaches. Unlike the outwardly expressive Fire and Wood children, the Earth child becomes distracted by internal thoughts, worrying that someone is mad at her. The increasing sense of detachment drives her to become clingier, disregarding boundaries and further alienating her from peers. During the "tween" years (ten to twelve years old), when social niches are solidifying, Earth children are particularly vulnerable to all the dangers of peer pressure.

When the puppy heart dominates the Earth child's attention, it manifests as difficulty prioritizing. Indecision and disorganization become the hallmarks of this type of ADHD. "If I sit with you, she's going to be upset; if I sit with her, you will be upset." Likewise, "If I start my math homework, I won't have time to do my English, but if I do my English I won't finish my math." Aggravating their insecurity, Earth children are often harshly judged for their need for attachment in a society that favors individuality and independence.

Sleep and the Earth Child

The Earth child will find it hard to fall asleep when she cannot turn off her mind. This is a sign that the puppy heart is overriding frog-heart rhythms. The longer she stays awake, the more she worries about not getting enough sleep. It's not uncommon to find the Earth child in your room at 2 a.m. saying, "Mommy, I can't sleep," just to make contact.

Characteristics of the Earth Child

Tuned In (Big Hearted)	Tuned Out (Puppy Hearted)	Physical Signs of Tuning Out
"The True Caregiver" The power of presence Attracted to attachments Nonlinear thinker Natural concern for others Learns by relationships Makes decisions by committee Content to be part of group Archetype: The Peacemaker	"The Worrier" Obsessive thinking Distracted by separation Disorganized, indecisive Excessive socializing Has trouble with boundaries Difficulty working alone Clingy, whiny, needy	Indigestion Vague stomachaches Overeating Weight problems Cravings: sweets, carbohydrates Fears: separation, not fitting in Cry: *I will if you do!*

The Metal Child

Autumn is the season that follows the harvest of Earth. This is the time when the fruit that wasn't picked or eaten drops to the ground, dries out, and thickens its skin in order to protect the precious seeds within. In Five Phase Correspondence, Metal reflects this power of the surface to become a shield. We feel the cooler, drier air on our skin. Leaves stiffen and drop from the trees, revealing the intricate structure of the forest; suddenly we see the logic of branching patterns in the trees. Perennials die back, showing the design of garden walls and walks. The patterns revealed in autumn offer us a glimpse of the rhyme and reason of nature. Its color is the bright white light that clarifies precise patterns and boundaries. We feel it in the righteous rhythm of our breath. As nights grow longer and days grow shorter, we are reminded of the passage of time. In the microcosm of our day, this is reflected in the beauty of the sunset. With a trace of sorrow, we say good-bye to the day.

The Metal Child Tuned In

The Metal child understands the world through its rhythms and reasons. She recognizes patterns where others may not see them. There is a truth in patterns that is prized by the Metal child. Tuned in, the treasure of her big heart shines, enabling her to become a true judge in the world by weighing all sides of an argument. Her power of attention lies in precision. Paying close attention to detail, she knows the world through its structure, form, and logic. Black, white, black, white...the next *must* be black. The Metal child finds comfort in routine and consistency. This is how she processes what is happening around her. Metal children have an amazing aesthetic sense. They are drawn to patterns and puzzles; the more detail, the more attraction. As babies, Metal children feel most secure when schedules are consistent. It's not uncommon to find a Metal child delaying reaching a developmental milestone until she has perfected it. Metal children are particular in the ways they play, regardless of what other children are doing. This independent mind, having a strong respect for boundaries, contrasts with that of the Wood child's pushing and the Earth child's need to fit in. The archetype of Metal is the alchemist, who can transform matter because she sees the logic in the details. Architects like Frank Lloyd Wright and scientists like Sir Isaac Newton have classic Metal sensibilities, creating beauty out of patterns.

Physically, Metal children may appear stiff, holding themselves poised in odd positions. They may avoid direct eye contact. Their tastes may seem finicky but they are particularly refined for young children.

Metal children often excel in subjects that require pattern identification and sequencing, like writing, drawing, music, and math. They may show a particular attraction to letters at early ages. The Metal child has an innate sense of right and wrong and may think in concrete terms that reduce matters to black and white. Since the world rarely goes according to plan, this is when a Metal child can easily get stuck.

Metal Attractions/Distractions

Metal children are attracted to order and distracted by disorder. They are focused on connecting the dots and finding patterns. This may take precedence over whatever else is going on around them, particularly social interactions, which can seem simply too inconsistent to be bothered with. It is inconsistency and disorder that undermine their sense of security.

The Metal Child Tuned Out

When the Metal child feels insecure, she tends to become more rigid. When inconsistency is overwhelming, her puppy heart barks out for order. This is how the power of precision becomes compulsive. In school, the Metal child is faced with a new set of rules that may challenge her own sense of right and wrong. Some Metal children find it difficult to deal with the chaos of social-group dynamics. But unlike the other types of ADHD, the Metal child's tendency is to hyperfocus when overstressed. She finds it increasingly hard to "see the forest for the trees." Getting stuck on inconsistencies, being unable to let them go, she tunes out what's going on with the group. This can set up a vicious cycle: the more hyperfocused, the more ostracized she is for being too rigid. Then this feeling of being misunderstood only drives her into a more rigid state. As the Metal child struggles to maintain a sense of order, transitions become more threatening. In such an amplified state, she becomes more disappointed by the tiniest inconsistencies. Disappointment leads to self-righteousness in a desperate attempt to compensate. This can be extremely frustrating for parents and teachers. As insecurity mounts, she becomes hypersensitive to criticism. Mistakes take on an amplified sense of condemnation and shame. A teacher who is pushing the class to move faster may find the Metal child slowing the class down with her need for perfection. In such a hyperfocused state, she finds it impossible to shift attention naturally.

The Metal child may begin exhibiting ritualistic behaviors as a way of maintaining some sense of order in the face of perceived chaos. In extreme cases, this can manifest physically as facial tics, which increase the more she tries to control things. Other physical signs of the Metal child's imbalance with her environment include eczema, wheezing, and constipation—all signs of an inability to relax and let go. During the teen years, the insecure Metal child is particularly at risk for compulsive behaviors such as eating disorders.

Sleep and the Metal Child

Metal children are easily stressed by transitions, making sleep a particularly challenging time for them if there is no routine. Often, the more insecure the Metal child is, the more elaborate the bedtime routine becomes, much to the frustration of her parents.

Characteristics of the Metal Child

Tuned In (Big Hearted)	Tuned Out (Puppy Hearted)	Physical Signs of Tuning Out
"The True Judge"	"The Perfectionist"	Stiff joints, muscles
Attracted to order and patterns	Distracted by disorder	Dry skin or hair
The power of precision	Rigidity	Wheezing or constipation
Attention to detail	Hyperfocused	Hypersensitivities
Love of numbers and letters	Gets stuck on mistakes	Poor circulation, easily cold
Innate aesthetic sense	Easily insulted	Sensitive to smells, tastes
Innate sense of right and wrong	Self-righteous	Cravings: has unusual predilections, craves rich foods
Natural sense of rhythm, timing	Easily disappointed	Fears: being wrong, making mistakes, boundaries being invaded
Strong sense of justice	Blames others	Cry: *"That's not right!"*
Finds security in routine	Ritualistic, compulsive,	
Concrete thinker	Has difficulty imagining choices	
Archetype: The Alchemist	Can't see forest for the trees	

The Water Child

Winter is the time when nature seems to completely turn inward, as if the world has gone to sleep. Look in the garden and all you see is snow and a few dead sticks. But beneath the surface, there is a rich life going on. Roots are growing, animals are hibernating, bulbs are storing up their concentrated energy for next year's growth. But we don't have access to it. Winter is the time for quiet regeneration and introspection. It's the time of year when one sits by the fire and reads a good book. It's a time for private contemplation, and it is no wonder that so many holy festivals take place in the dead of winter. At the solstice, the longest night, we celebrate the mystery of life's essence and consider the deep questions: Where do we come from? Where are we going? Water represents all this deep mystery. Everything lies hidden beneath the snow. It's dark and quiet at the bottom of the sea. The color of water is dark blue or black. Its light is like the black light whose eerie glow reveals strange shapes and shadows. Groping in the dark, this wonder tinged with dread raises the hairs on the back of our neck. We say we feel it in our bones.

The Water Child Tuned In

As with the activity that characterizes winter, it's not always easy to see what's going on in the mind of the Water child. Water children are our deep thinkers, our dreamers. They have a profound imagination as deep as the blue sea. Tuned in to the world, the treasure of their big heart shines, enabling them to become true sages in the world. Their power of attention lies in their total "immersion" in things. Water children can get so lost in their own inner explorations that they lose all track of time. As babies, they're sometimes called "old souls." We cannot imagine what they are thinking behind those deep, penetrating stares. As they get older, they dance to the beat of a different drummer. They seek meaning in their private, inner explorations. The archetype of Water is the philosopher, the Renaissance man. Leonardo da Vinci is a classic example of a Water temperament. When he died they found volumes of notebooks, written backward, of his studies of botany, anatomy, painting, the flight of birds, fantasy inventions, and of course the challenge of capturing a mysterious smile on a woman's face. But he never thought to publish these writings and sketches. They were private explorations. His inner world was what mattered most.

Water children may develop slowly, they may walk late ("Who needs to walk when I can examine my belly button?"), they may speak late ("Who needs to speak when words cannot describe the infinite truths of life?"), and they may even grow slowly. This can be a great concern for parents. Many Water children end up being evaluated for developmental services to help them adjust to our world. They sometimes need outside help to stay in tune with our modern, scheduled life. Curiously, when secure, Water children can be immersed in their own world and still know exactly what's going on around them.

Time is the great challenge for the Water child. She looks at time as if it were infinite. Living by the artificial clock puts great pressure on her. Doing things on time can be the source of the Water child's insecurity. Nowhere is this pressure felt more acutely than in school. That's when we see the Water child increasingly tuning out.

Water Attractions/Distractions

Water children are attracted to time's infinite mystery and distracted by the urgency of everyday affairs. They have unusual, quirky interests that can make them seem odd to their peers. Because they're deeply immersed in their explorations, it's sometimes difficult for others to connect with them, and this becomes a great source of stress in their lives.

The Water Child Tuned Out

Dancing to the beat of a different drummer is fine unless that beat is so slow, so barely audible that no one else hears it. Being misunderstood is a great source of stress for the Water child. This likelihood is amplified in the fast-paced classroom. Like the stream winding its way down the mountain, the Water child never seems to go in straight lines, taking her time, unperturbed by outside pressures. She may never finish her work, much to the dismay of the teacher. Under the world's pressures she simply goes deeper into her own world. The more the Water child struggles with the pressures of time in the classroom, the further she falls behind. There's a risk that she'll eventually drown in the workload until she becomes apathetic. Her own fertile imagination becomes her distraction. Daydreaming or looking out the window, she has no clue what's going on in the classroom. Her stubbornness is different from the Metal child's righteous refusal to do things a different way. For the Water child, it is a willful determination to stay in her own world. This is a sure sign that her puppy heart is dominating. Just as water has the tendency to settle, Water children often lose all motivation when they feel insecure. Their power of immersion can turn into withdrawal, and this can be infuriating for any parent or teacher who is trying to get them going. Just getting dressed in the morning can take forever. In school, because teachers themselves are under enormous pressure to keep the class moving forward, the Water child appears to drag the class down. Misunderstood, they are often referred for neurologic evaluation. These steps are rarely fruitful. After all, there really is no standard by which the Water child can be measured!

For the Water child, it is time itself that is the stressor in their lives. Even the smallest assignment takes forever to complete. These children are often classified by conventional psychiatrists as having "inattentive type ADD." They are not hyperactive or impulsive; on the contrary, they're barely moving.

Being old souls, Water children have difficulty playing the silly games other children play. Being frequently misunderstood, the Water child tends to withdraw. Unable to make contact, she becomes a loner. Finding it difficult to connect and get feedback, her self-esteem drops, resulting in long-standing denial, depression, and isolation.

Sleep and the Water Child

Water children often have trouble waking up in the morning. They prefer the privacy of their rooms and will spend long hours alone. They often become "night owls," doing their best work long after everyone else has gone to sleep. Some Water children are paralyzed by deep-seated fears that keep them awake, though they may be unable to talk to anyone about them.

Characteristics of the Water Child

Tuned In (Big Hearted)	Tuned Out (Puppy Hearted)	Physical Signs of Tuning Out
"The True Sage"	"The Daydreamer"	Low physical stamina,
The power of	Withdrawn, detached	Failure to thrive
immersion	Head in the clouds	Deterioration of teeth,
Deep thinker	Negative thoughts	gums
Precocious knowledge,	Forgetful	Backaches
memory	Oppositional	Cravings: salty, meats,
Dances to different	Socially isolated	hot foods
drummer	Morose, dark, moody	Fears: death,
Strong-willed	Difficulty expressing	vulnerability
Comfortable being	ideas	Cry: *"You can't make*
alone	Unable to finish	*me!"*
Interest in mystery and	anything	
magic	Hopeless, prone to	
Tends to be quiet	depression	
Takes time doing things	Apathetic, difficult to	
Great imagination	motivate	
Archetype: The		
Philosopher		

The Five Types of ADHD

The purpose of this chapter is to honor our diversity and to discover the unique way your child is paying attention to the world. When conditions support your child's nature, she is able to pay attention effectively, expanding the big heart and promoting deeper understanding, empathy, imagination, and self-regulation. This is what every parent I meet wants for their child.

When conditions don't support your child's nature, we hear the barking puppy of Wood, Fire, Earth, Metal, or Water telling us she's insecure. If you look carefully, all five of these adaptive styles have symptoms of ADHD when their puppy heart is dominating the scene. These then are the Five Types of ADHD (see chart).

Wood Child	Fire Child	Earth Child	Metal Child	Water Child
Frustrated	Impulsive	Worried	Rigid	Withdrawn
Hyperactive	Silly	Obsessive	Hyperfocused	Daydreaming
Angry	Lazy	Disorganized	Stuck	Slow
Explosive	Bored	Indecisive	Compulsive	Apathetic

One Size Does Not Fit All

Treating all five types of ADHD as if they are the same is bad medicine and very dangerous. The Wood child can't pay attention because she needs to escape and can't sit still. The Fire child can't pay attention because her heightened sensitivity makes her impulsive. The Earth child can't pay attention because she's so worried that she can't decide anything. The Metal child can't pay attention because she's stuck on the details and can't go with the flow of the class. And the Water child can't pay attention because she has escaped into her own inner world. Each of these is a cry for help.

Put them all on the same medication and this is what happens:

For the Wood child, it may seem like a miracle, temporarily. Suddenly the child is totally focused on what the teacher is saying. Why? Because Wood children love *speed*. They love the feeling stimulants give. The medication creates a kind of "chemical emergency" that makes the classroom a matter of life and death, as thrilling perhaps as those video games she so loves to play. The problem is that they tend to adapt very quickly to the effects, and the dose has to be raised to maintain that same level of thrill in order to keep them focused. This progressive ramping up can result in medication levels in which toxic symptoms like headaches, palpitations, weight loss, and insomnia require different medications.

When the Fire child is given stimulant medications, it may have a modest effect on attention but nobody likes what it does to her personality. Parents complain that it takes away her charm, the very characteristic that everyone loves about her. The Fire child herself often doesn't like the feeling she has on the medications. She may complain that it makes her agitated or causes heart palpitations. Medication can dampen the Fire child's light. As one child simply put it, "It takes the carnival away; it makes everything seem so dull."

The Earth child is not paying attention because she's overthinking. Placing her on these medications only makes her more anxious, causing increased somatic signs of stress such as sleeplessness and stomachaches.

Place the Metal child on stimulants and it only increases her already hyperfocused state. If before she couldn't see the forest for the trees, now she can't see the trees for the bark! The medications simply amplify her rigidity, bringing out motor tics and worsening compulsive behaviors.

When you give the Water child stimulant medications, the chemical speed can have the opposite effect, pushing her even further into her own world. It can amplify feelings of detachment from the world and place her at risk for depression and thoughts of suicide.

It's fascinating to note that looking at the warnings listed on the labels for stimulant medications used in ADHD will reveal all these symptoms. A certain percentage of children will develop headaches, palpitations, personality changes, stomachaches, compulsive behaviors, tics, and even suicidal ideation. But no one ever explains *which* kids are at risk for each of these side effects! It's as if lightning simply strikes some poor kids. That is simply not scientific and poses an unacceptable risk. Medicating a child without knowing the risks specific to that child is just like treating fever without knowing the underlying causes. It's just bad medicine. On the other hand, once you understand your child's nature, you can discover more personal and practical ways to improve your child's attention.

The beauty of the Five Phase model is that it embraces our diversity. One style of adapting is not necessarily better than the others. We need them all in our world. Children have different predilections and develop at different rates, and each adaptive style serves an important purpose in our society. Our ancestors knew the importance of this. Every child has something to offer. When I work with a child and she discovers what her secret powers are, it opens up a whole new way of seeing her purpose in the world. The trick is finding the optimal way of cultivating these powers and developing the kind of emotional regulation that brings out your child's talents. As we will see in the next chapter, once you know who your child is, we can map out ways to help you help your child.

Confused about Your Child's Nature?

Some parents may have difficulty figuring out which of the five natures most resembles their child. For others it may be obvious. Remember, we each have aspects of all five forces of nature. Ultimately it's the mix of these that characterize our individuality. No one is pure Fire or pure Water. Circumstances bring out qualities of a specific nature. Some children (and parents) may show signs of two forces of nature, and this is important information that sheds light on conflicts within their lives. Mixed natures are particularly evident as we get older and learn to adopt other qualities to help us survive. To get started, it's best to look for the predominant way your child adapts to the stressors she meets in the world. You can utilize recommendations made for other adaptive styles. If you're still having trouble figuring out your child's nature, here are a few tips:

What is my child's nature?

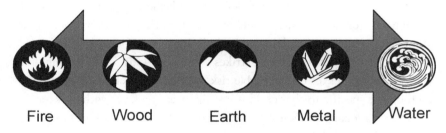

Fire   Wood   Earth   Metal   Water

The Spectrum of Five Natures

1. The seasons exist on a spectrum: summer has the longest days and is the hottest while winter has the longest nights and is the coldest. As you can see from the diagram above, the five natures reflect this spectrum as well, with Fire (the most outgoing) on one end and Water (the most introspective) on the other. Which end of the spectrum is your child on? Is your child more distracted by external or internal stimuli? Wood and Fire are more outwardly stimulated. On

the other end, Water and Metal are focused on internal stimuli. The Earth child sits somewhere in the middle, sometimes caught up by the outside world, sometimes more distracted by inner thoughts. Because Earth children are so concerned about fitting in, they can sometimes be difficult to identify. Like chameleons, they often take on the characteristics of those around them. Which end of the spectrum does your child gravitate toward? If you really can't figure out your child's nature, perhaps she is an Earth child.

2. Don't get confused if your child has some features that don't fit perfectly into one category. As we'll see in the coming chapters, this may actually be a clue to where your child is struggling. Look for the most predominant features in your child.

3. Remember to look at what your child is interested in, not just what she's distracted by. Her passions can often serve as clues pointing you toward identifying her powers of attention. Remember that the five types of ADHD are simply an amplification of these powers.

4. Remember that we, as parents, tend to color our impressions of who our child is through our own subjective lens. We may have specific expectations about how a child should behave. It's not uncommon to expect our children to be little versions of ourselves. However, our kids rarely turn out as photocopies of us, and missing their differences can be a great source of confusion and misunderstanding.

5. If you are still having trouble figuring out your child's nature, consider having a friend or another family member look at the chart to help you. You can also download a teacher questionnaire at www.stephencowanmd.com.

6. Below are some comparisons that may help you differentiate among the five natures.

Comparisons among the Five Natures

Water and Wood Tuned In Both have a passion to explore	Water Tunes in quietly, inwardly	Wood Tunes in actively, outwardly
Water and Wood Tuned Out Both become loners	Withdraws	Pushes back
Wood and Fire Tuned In Both crave excitement	Wood Directed toward winning	Fire Directed toward fun
Wood and Fire Tuned Out Both become agitated	It's never enough Easily frustrated	Easily overstimulated Tends to panic
Fire and Earth Tuned In Both like contact	Fire Actively engaged in exploring contact	Earth Content with sustained connection
Fire and Earth Tuned Out Both panic at separation	Impulsively moves on Easily distracted by sensations	Worries about maintaining contact Easily obsessed
Earth and Metal Tuned In Both like predictability	Earth Security in context	Metal Security in routine
Earth and Metal Tuned Out Both overthink	Obsessed about the whole (context) Easily disorganized by details	Obsessed with the parts Loses sight of the whole

Metal and Water Tuned In Both happy to be alone	Metal Needs rhythm and routine	Water Needs free time, no routine
Metal and Water Tuned Out Both get very quiet	Broods about right and wrong Gets lost in details Easily compulsive, stuck on things	Escapes in imagination Gets lost in own world Loses motivation Becomes disoriented and afraid

Strong Contrasting Natures

Fire and Metal	Fire Seeks intensity Attracted to novelty Easily bored with monotony	Metal Dislikes intensity Likes things to be the same Overwhelmed by change
Water and Fire	Water Likes to be alone	Fire Dislikes being alone
Metal and Wood	Metal Holds back	Wood Needs to advance
Wood and Earth	Wood Pushes in contact	Earth Content in contact
Earth and Water	Earth Wants contact	Water Tends to isolate

Chapter 5

Mapping Solutions for Your Child

As we've seen, none of us lives in a vacuum. How we focus and what we focus on are shaped by who we are, our relationships, and our experiences. Understanding the context of your child's life lies at the heart of this holistic approach. The five types of ADHD give you a clue to what your child's nature is. Gaining an understanding of your child's nature will help you understand how to help him improve his attention. For example, if you happen to have a child whose impulsivity and dramatic mood swings are consistent with Fire-type ADHD, then we can create a strategy to help him develop the big-hearted attention of a Fire child.

Once you have a good sense of your child's nature, you can begin to map out ways to shape your child's environment so that he can become a master of attention in any situation. Remember, nature favors diversity. When the environment encourages your child to see the big picture, he has access to a broader range of emotional responses to changing circumstances. This is what I mean by "diversity." Your child is free to choose from a number of responses to a stressor. This allows him to adapt with creativity, freeing him from the tendency to get stuck in only one puppy reaction. We can think of the equation like this:

> Optimum stress = Tuning in to big picture = Embracing diversity
>
> Non-optimum stress = Tuning out the world = Barking puppy

The relationship between context and attention goes both ways. The inability to experience diverse emotional states creates stress in the environment, too. That's what happens when a child is disruptive in a classroom. To break these vicious cycles we must support the security of the puppy heart while expanding the big heart. This is the key to your child's happiness and success. In this chapter, we will discuss the general approach to developing your child's big-hearted attention. In the following chapters, I will discuss individual strategies for each of the five types of ADHD.

Know Your Own Heart

The process begins by understanding your own strengths as a caregiver. Who are *you* in the big picture? Parents and teachers play key roles in developing a child's unique set of skills and talents. Take the time to examine your own nature. I find it amazing how often parents have the exact qualities their children need in order to grow. You may just need to identify them. Parents sometimes say: "It's not about me. It's my child who has the problem with attention here!" While this book is not about blaming parents for their children's problems, it *is* about making them part of the solution. Discovering how to cultivate your own nature makes you an active participant in your child's future. That's how you become the perfect medicine for your child. But it takes time and practice to look at yourself.

An Interplay of Forces

The ancient Chinese modeled their way of understanding health on the relationships among the five forces of nature. No force exists independently of the others, just as no season can exist alone. Nothing is ever absolute or taken out of context. We can use these relationships to find practical ways of correcting imbalances in your child's behavior.

For many caregivers, simply discovering the unique qualities of their child is enough to shift expectations. They see their child in a different light and begin to understand what's needed to create a safe haven for that child. Embracing tolerance for our diversity is the true power of love. Remember, the purpose is to meet your child where he is, to embrace his unique nature in order to shape an environment that promotes the kind of security that he requires. It is only then that you can gradually empower him to expand his big heart. To do this, I suggest following the following four steps:

1. Feeding the puppy heart

2. Training the puppy heart

3. Expanding the big heart

4. Mastering the big heart

Feeding the Puppy Heart: Nourishing Security

Before you can expect your child to pay attention calmly, you have to understand what's needed to create a more secure base for him to grow in. Just as the seasons turn in sequence, so do the five forces "feed" each other in a predictable cycle that ensures growth and security. To feed your child's puppy heart:

Wood Feeds Fire: Wood is the fuel for fire (just as spring becomes summer).

Fire Feeds Earth: Ash becomes earth (just as summer becomes harvest).

Earth Feeds Metal: Earth feeds metals (just as harvest becomes autumn).

Metal Feeds Water: From the top of a mountain comes water (just as autumn becomes winter).

Water Feeds Wood: The melting snow makes the forest grow (just as winter becomes spring).

The Nourishing Cycle

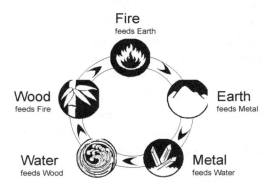

This is called the *nourishing cycle* of life (see diagram). You don't need a sophisticated experiment to prove this. All the evidence is right outside your window. Each season nourishes the next. Simply identifying your child's nature allows you to find the force that feeds it (comes before it on the diagram). We can use those powers to bring greater intimacy between your child and his surroundings. Often nonverbal cues like body language can generate a greater sense of security, allowing your child to catch a glimpse of what calm attention actually feels like. Doing so, he can begin to make the connection between his feelings and reactions. For example, Fire feeds Earth. An Earth child who is overly anxious needs support from Fire (in the form of compassionate humor) to help lighten his mood and strengthen feelings of being connected (his natural interest). This is taking care of "me first" before expecting your child to use the executive functions of the big heart.

Training the Puppy Heart: Directing a Secure Path

Life is not just about nourishing. By itself, feeding can make things grow out of control. The purpose is not to indulge your child's puppy heart. A puppy needs training if he's going to live in your house. In nature there are always regulating forces that balance the exuberance of growth. These are extremely powerful and require care. In training however, we don't want to kill your child's spirit. This is where the real power of "less is love" becomes extremely important. You can map out the counterbalancing forces in your child's life:

Water Regulates Fire: A little water controls fire, allowing it to function efficiently. Too much puts it out.

Wood Regulates Earth: A little wood contains the earth, preventing landslides. Too much breaks it apart, making it impossible to grow anything.

Fire Regulates Metal: A little fire tempers metal, so that it can be shaped into something useful. Too much makes a molten mess.

Earth Regulates Water: A little earth channels water through canals and irrigation ditches. Too much muddies water's clarity, blocking its flow.

Metal Regulates Wood: A little metal prunes a tree, giving it shape and making it more productive. Too much cuts it down like an axe.

This is the *regulating cycle* of life. Once you have begun to create a secure base, you can begin to direct your child's nature along a secure path so that he's not simply stuck in habitual overreactions. Having created opportunities for your child to experience moments of calm attention, we can now begin to create opportunities for emotional exchanges. Training a puppy means using repetition and reward to promote dependable behavior. When the puppy heart is insecure, it requires positive nonverbal feedback to encourage intimacy and counterbalance the urgency to bark. This deepens trust in relationships and opens opportunities to cope with transitions and sharing. But this is tricky business. Don't just push your agenda. Too many restrictions simply suppress your child's natural affinities. Instead, we can use his interests to gradually move him toward an experience of a wider range of emotional states. For example, a Wood child who loves movement but is hyperactive needs just enough of Metal's structure as consistent feedback to help him realize that he's not the center of the world without feeling threatened. Channeling his immense energy within a predictable set of consequences (Metal), such as competitive sports, will give him the opportunity to share his strengths with others.

The Regulating Cycle

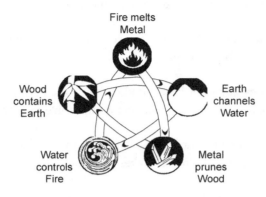

Fire melts
Metal

Wood
contains
Earth

Earth
channels
Water

Water
controls
Fire

Metal
prunes
Wood

Finding the right balance between feeding and training is mediated by your own big-hearted love for your child. Be patient. Feeding and training can take some time. Your love ensures that you will see the world from your child's perspective and use just the right amount of force to effectively engage his nature.

Expanding the Big Heart: Offering an Outlet to Diversity

When a child is in an insecure state, he can feel emotionally trapped. The barking puppy needs a way out. The purpose of feeding and training is not to suppress your child's emotions. Remember, emotions are not bad. They are just an expression of your child's state of security. But your child is not just a dog. Once your child has learned to read your nonverbal cues encouraging states of calm attention, we can create opportunities to open up his big heart, using words to bring greater awareness to shifting emotional states. You can do this by labeling different emotional states as they are happening. Catching your child laughing or sad, frustrated or anxious, and labeling these for him without judgment brings greater perspective to shifts in feelings. This allows him to detect subtle shades of feelings as they are beginning, rather than simply jumping to extremes. This begins by offering an outlet for your child to experience big-heartedness.

To map a way out for your child, look at the force that follows your child's nature. This is the direction of your child's life. In a sense, it is his destiny and brings deeper meaning and purpose to his nature.

The outlet for **Wood** is **Fire.**

The outlet for **Fire** is **Earth.**

The outlet for **Earth** is **Metal.**

The outlet for **Metal** is **Water.**

The outlet for **Water** is **Wood.**

For example, we know that Wood is destined to be fuel for Fire, bringing heat and light to the world. Likewise, a Wood child's intense drive can find an outlet in such Fire activities as performance, in which he learns to express himself in more refined ways and gets feedback without overreacting. By practicing expanding his big heart, he begins to manifest his destiny, experiencing what it feels like to be a true hero to the world.

Creating an Outlet: Expanding the Big Picture

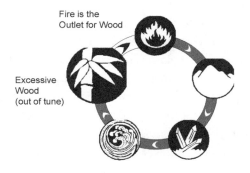

Fire is the
Outlet for Wood

Excessive
Wood
(out of tune)

Mastering the Big Heart: Developing Self-Reflection

Once your child has found a stronger sense of security and you've given him an outlet to identify big-heartedness and use a range of emotions, he is now ready to begin mastering his own self-awareness. Mastering the big heart is a gradual process. Your child can use his powers of imagination to see himself in a larger context. Activities that encourage your child to recognize the effect he is having on others make up a key component of this stage. To understand this larger perspective, you need to be aware of specific relationships that your child is prone to disrupt when out of control:

Wood disrupts **Earth.**

Fire disrupts **Metal.**

Earth disrupts **Water.**

Metal disrupts **Wood.**

Water disrupts **Fire.**

For example, a Fire child is prone to disrupting the order (Metal) of a classroom if his excitability is too excessive, while a Water child is prone to disrupting the silliness (Fire) of a group activity if his seriousness is excessive. Gaining a broader perspective of the effects one is having on others begins by getting your child to notice the way his own emotions change from day to day. You can create opportunities for your child to compare his emotional states between yesterday and today. From this he can begin to imagine how he might feel tomorrow. He then begins to connect specific situations and people to his own moods and behaviors. This kind of self-reflection enables your child to consider things from another's point of view as well. Using strategies like role-playing, painting, writing, and mindfulness meditation will allow your child to put his feelings in context and learn to express his emotions with greater clarity and imagination, allowing others to understand him better. With greater communication comes greater confidence and less need for the intense puppy-hearted impulses and ADHD reactions. Developing true mastery of the big heart allows your child to become a virtuoso of his talents, solving problems with greater freedom and creativity. You will find specific ways to utilize these four steps for each of the five types of ADHD in the chapters that follow.

Using the Five Phases Therapeutically

Over the years, I discovered innovative ways to use the Five Phases Correspondences to create practical therapeutic interventions that help children develop their attention. Each of the five phases has its own power to transform. Once you understand your child's nature, you can use specific activities from each of the phases to feed, train, expand, and help your child master his attention. Remember, the point of this book is that one size does not fit all. For example, Wood activites may be useful in feeding the puppy heart of the Fire child or regulating the puppy heart of the Earth child. While many of these activities may be beneficial for all children, the sequence needs to be specific for each child's nature. We must always start by creating a greater sense of security (feeding the puppy heart) before we can consider developing self-reflection (mastering the big heart). Below is a quick primer for parents that offers examples of a range of activities that relate to each of the five phases. These can be incorporated into the strategy sequence that is specific to your child's nature.

Strategies for Mastering Attention

Wood Child	Fire Child	Earth Child	Metal Child	Water Child
Water feeds	Wood feeds	Fire feeds	Earth feeds	Metal feeds
Metal trains	Water trains	Wood trains	Fire trains	Earth trains
Fire expands	Earth	Metal	Water	Wood
Earth	expands	expands	expands	expands
masters	Metal	Water	Wood	Fire masters
	masters	masters	masters	

WOOD ACTIVITIES

These activities encourage physical movement, exploration, trailblazing, tracking, pushing boundaries, decision making, courage, and the determination to reach goals and develop the power of flow.

- **Physical Exercise:** Encourages kinesthetic learning. (Try hiking, martial arts, or yoga.)

- **Physical Therapy:** Improves body awareness and range of motion.

- **Vision Therapy:** Research has shown that eye-movement problems can be associated with ADHD (Granet et al. 2005). Simple exercises can help enhance visual tracking and focus.

- **"I Spy" Game:** Helps certain children become more aware of the diversity in physical space.

- **Spending Time in Nature:** Several studies have shown that spending time in nature can help with attention (Kuo and Taylor 2004) and improve a child's engagement in nonlinear physical relationships with the world.

- **Diet:** Wood is represented by muscle. Protein-rich foods are best for children whose metabolism requires longer-burning fuel.

- **Adventure Games:** Anything that enhances the spirit of adventure (travel, camping) helps certain children improve their kinesthetic learning skills.

- **Building:** Certain children benefit from doing more work with their hands. This helps develop spatial awareness in the world.

FIRE ACTIVITIES

Try these activities to help your child lighten his mood with warmth, humor, and joy. They encourage diversity through play, regulation through sensory experience, and expressivity through high engagement with the changing world.

- **Play-Acting and Performance:** Help develop a wide range of expression.

- **Humor and Silliness Play:** Help loosen rigid behaviors and reduce stress.

- **Speech Therapy:** The Fire phase is associated with verbal communication.

- **Biofeedback (emWave):** Fire is associated with the heart. This feedback device brings the pulse and respiration into a coherent rhythm, which studies have shown can enhance attention (Lloyd, Brett, and Wesnes 2010).

- **Sensory Integration:** When the puppy heart is dominating attention, the range of sensory awareness is narrow and amplified. Sensory-integration techniques help improve a child's regulation of sensory input, thereby expanding the range of sensory awareness that is crucial for calm attention.

- **Trusting Intuition:** Learning to trust one's feelings without being overwhelmed by them requires the ability to regulate emotional states. This opens up the possibility for greater creativity in solving problems.

- **"I Spy Something New":** Pick a familiar room and take turns seeing how many things you can find that are new, even if it's the smallest change in position of an object. This activity develops more acute attention to changes in the environment, brings a new perspective, connects your child to his environment, and opens new relationships with the world.

- **Travel:** Helps child embrace diversity and brings larger context to awareness.

EARTH ACTIVITIES

These help your child integrate information about the world, develop relationships, maintain contact, and promote harmony.

- **Eating (What, Where, When, How):** Food is the most basic process of information processing. Try playing a game with your child before eating (or while preparing a meal), taking turns noticing textures, tastes, colors, and smells of foods. You each get a point for noticing one thing. This helps your child develop a more refined sense of attention and actually stimulates hunger.

- **The "I'm Hungry 1-2-3" Game:** At the start of a meal, ask your child how hungry he is (1 = a lot, 3 = not at all). In the middle of the meal, ask your child if he can tell if his stomach is 1 = still empty, 2 = half full, or 3 = full. Practice gradually improving his attention to his feelings. This has been shown to help develop emotional regulation.

- **Cooking:** Promotes attention to sequence and process (recipes) and expands your child's awareness of diverse patterns, textures, and smells.

- **Five Phase Flavors:** Chinese medicine has developed an elaborate system for assigning flavors and specific foods to each phase (Wood-sour, Fire-bitter, Earth-sweet, Metal-pungent, Water-salty). These can be used therapeutically in specific situations to expand experience of diversity and enhance attention. (See appendix for more on the Five Phases of food.)

- **Singing Together (Harmonizing):** Earth is associated with the sound of singing. The activity of harmonizing promotes attention to a greater range of expression and helps your child focus on regulating his own voice and learning to blend it with others. This sets the stage for more sophisticated ways of exchanging ideas.

- **Learning through Relationships:** When information is placed in context, it can be retained more effectively. It is through the connections between pieces of information that deeper meaning can be gained.

- **Analogic Reasoning:** The ability to use metaphors is an important part of the big heart executive function. Analogies allow a child to see connections between seemingly disparate ideas. Developing these skills through metaphor has been shown to improve attention, comprehension, and problem solving (Weatherholt et al. 2006).

- **Social-Skills Classes:** Strengthen relationships and help develop trust and tolerance.

- **Chanting:** Improves focus and reduces stress. Chanting is an ancient practice used in many traditional cultures to integrate mind and body. Using repeated sounds brings together the elements of rhythm (Metal) and resonance (Earth) while reducing the stress of over-thinking and opening up an experience of intuition (Fire). (I'll discuss chanting further in the following chapters on the individual natures.)

METAL ACTIVITIES

These techniques, games, and tools promote a sense of order, consistency, and rhythm. Metal's power lies in structure and sequence with a special attention to patterns and detail.

- **The Time Game:** I often say that minutes were invented by the Metal-natured to help us stay organized. Have your child time simple tasks around the house, like brushing his teeth. Then see whether your child can guess what five minutes actually feels like. Gradually, he will master the feeling of longer intervals. This game improves organization skills and comes in handy in timed activities like examinations.

- **Mapping the Day:** Mapping out your child's day helps orient him to the big picture, improving his sense of order and thus reducing anxiety. See the diagram for an example of what your child's Day Map might look like. You can map homework in the same way.

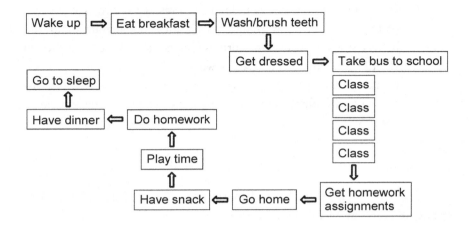

- **Reward Charts:** Training any puppy requires repetition and rewards. Set up a positive reward chart that focuses on your child's ability to shift from wild to calmer attention. This helps expand the big heart and improve emotional regulation. (I'll provide more information on positive rewards in the following chapters.)

- **The Homework Game:** There is nothing that makes the puppy heart bark louder than homework. Getting homework done is impossible without motivation. Motivating your child requires consistency (Metal) and reward (Fire).

  1. Start simply. Remember, nobody starts a game at level 4. Don't overwhelm your child. Try to motivate one thing at a time (for instance, reward your child if he can estimate how long each subject is going to take him). Remember, the object of the game is to win, not lose.

  2. Decide on a reward. Everyone should agree on the reward before the game begins. This reduces any chance for bargaining at the end. Make rewards attractive, but avoid too many material things if possible. These may just stimulate the self-centered activity of the puppy heart. Activities that encourage time with your child help expand his big heart by deepening the bonds between you and are more memorable in the long run.

3. Establish a proxy reward. Using stickers, buttons, poker chips, or some other proxy to stand in for the reward offers your child a chance to work toward the real reward. He'll be cashing in his chips to get his prize.

4. Reward. The final reward comes when the child earns two proxy rewards consecutively. If your child succeeds one day and not the next, he has to start over on the third day. By promoting delayed gratification you are training your child to regulate his impulses.

5. Write up an agreement that states what the game is, how many chips or stickers the child needs to earn, and what the reward will be. When both of you sign the agreement, it affirms to your child that you're each playing the game by the same rules.

6. Don't break the rules. Be consistent if your want your child to trust you.

7. Once your child has shown that he can consistently win at level 1, he can move up to higher levels of the game. You may want to increase the difficulty by requiring three consecutive proxy rewards to get the final reward or by adding another skill.

- **Finding Patterns and Rhythms:** Both visual (model building, Legos, arts and crafts, ceramics, jewelry making, pattern books) and auditory (playing music, drumming, dancing) patterns develop trust in sequence, help release tension, and regulate attention.

- **Interactive Metronome:** This is a neuromotor therapy that synchronizes body movements (Wood) to rhythm (Metal), improving body awareness and timing. You can learn more about Interactive Metronome by visiting their website, which is listed in the resources at the end of the book.

- **Aromatherapy:** The sense of smell is associated with the Metal phase. Different essential oils can be used in baths or a vaporizer, or for massage (in vegetable oils or lotions) to stimulate memory, regulate emotions, and promote calm attention (see appendix for specific Five Phase aromatherapy recommendations for ADHD).

- **Breathing Exercises:** The lungs are associated with Metal in Chinese medicine. Breathing is the fundamental rhythm in our lives, and focusing on the breath has been shown to enhance calm attention and reduce distractibility. "Belly breathing" (see below) can be practiced before bed and then used in situations when a child is losing control. The practice will help to redirect attention and improve emotional regulation.

Basic Belly-Breathing Exercise: When I explain belly breathing to children, I talk about it as an ancient martial arts exercise that will give them secret powers. It's best to first practice at a quiet time, before bed for example. Basic belly breathing simply involves expanding the belly with inhalation and letting it go with exhalation. This helps your child shift attention away from the chest while he breathes (reducing fight-or-flight reactivity). Sometimes I'll place a small ball on the belly button to help keep a child focused on the belly. In qigong exercises, the area around the navel is called the *dan-tian*, "the field of heaven." It is a very important area for the generation and movement of *qi* (vital energy). (We'll look more deeply into qigong a bit later in the chapter.)

1. Have your child lie down and put one hand on his belly and the other on his chest.

2. Ask him to try breathing in (best through the nose) and filling up his belly like a balloon.

3. Have your child breathe out through his mouth, simply releasing his breath as if he were letting go of a balloon. This feeling of letting go is important in releasing tension.

4. Be patient. Your child is not used to this and it may be frustrating for him at first. In the beginning, start with one or two successful belly breaths and stop. Try to work your way up to twenty breaths each night.

5. This exercise can also be practiced standing up. Being able to belly breathe while standing will be useful when you need to help your

child calm down during or after a blowup. (You might share this technique with your child's teacher. It can be a great help during class, as long as the teacher is discreet in using it with your child.)

WATER ACTIVITIES

These promote the "power of immersion," quiet contemplation, deeper meaning, fantasy, and imagination.

- **Sleep:** The night corresponds to the Water phase in Chinese medicine and nourishes parasympathetic functions of resting and digesting to balance the fight-or-flight reactions of the sympathetic nervous system. Ensuring that your child gets enough sleep may be one of the most important ways to help him develop his attention. Dreams integrate the day's activities, thereby improving executive function and refreshing our perspective. Different children have different sleep requirements, and these will be discussed in the following chapters.

- **Fish Oils and Water:** Just like our planet, we are composed of approximately 70 percent water. Every cell requires water to function optimally, and adequate water intake is essential for healthy cognitive function. Omega-3 fish oils help make connections between the neocortex and limbic structures, enhancing regulation of the puppy heart. Studies have shown that these oils are as effective as stimulant medications in many children with ADHD (though they never tell you *which* kids benefit the most) (Sinn and Bryan 2007).

- **Swimming:** Regular swimming is a great way to relax the body and focus the mind.

- **Baths:** Having some quiet time to relax in warm water helps a child unwind and prepare for the transition between day and night. Epsom salts (magnesium sulfate) have a natural relaxing effect on the nervous system.

- **Poetry and Journaling:** Poetry helps condense ideas into simple meanings. Regular journaling helps develop the power of introspection.

- **Memory Games:** Enhancing memory gives a child access to a wider scope of information, which expands the big heart and helps your child engage in the world.

- **Craniosacral Therapy:** Water is associated with the bones in Chinese medicine. Craniosacral therapy involves subtle manipulation of the body that aims to balance the internal "craniosacral rhythms" of the cerebrospinal fluid. This can enhance calm focus for certain children with ADHD.

- **Mystery:** There are a number of fun mystery games available to help children develop this aspect of mind.

- **Religion:** Beliefs in greater powers help a child gain perspective, developing big heart virtues like humility, tolerance, empathy, and ethical behavior.

- **Adrenal Support:** The adrenals are associated with the Water phase (basic survival). I use a number of supplements in certain children to support their adrenals. These include the adaptogens (rhodiola, schizandra, ashwaganda, bacopa) and herbs (cordyceps, Siberian ginseng), as well as amino acids (l-tyrosine, l-theanine, taurine, 5-htp). I strongly recommend that you consult with a licensed herbalist or nutritionist before using any of these supplements.

- **Homeopathy:** This is a system of medicine developed over 100 years ago that utilizes extremely high dilutions of substances to neutralize specific symptoms. (See appendix for my Five Phase ADHD homeopathy.)

- **Flower Essences:** The first modern flower essences were developed by Dr. Edward Bach in the 1930s. Bach, a Water-natured character for sure, was a pioneer in holistic medicine. He held the radical perspective that all illness resulted from disharmony between mind and body. His original thirty-eight remedies have been greatly expanded in recent years. Flower essences are distilled from flowers and usually stored in alcohol. I recommend that you consult with a professional when using flower essences. (See appendix for specific Five Phase flower essences for ADHD and the resources section for additional information.)

Five Phase Qigong Exercises

Qigong exercises involve all five phases: movement, breath, sensory awareness, mindfulness, and insight. I have adapted these ancient exercises for children and find them very effective ways of improving attention. I tell children that these exercises can give them special secret powers, and, to a certain extent, this is actually true. As Master Ken Cohen describes in his wonderful book *The Way of Qigong*: "Qigong means working with the life energy, learning how to control the flow and distribution of qi to improve the health and harmony of mind and body" (Cohen 1997, 3). The intention in using these exercises is to help children learn how to master their unique powers and thus learn to be more fully present in the world. Remember, the key is starting small and gradually increasing the frequency and difficulty of these exercises. Less is more, if practiced every day. I will be discussing individual exercises for each of the five types in the following chapters.

Acupuncture and Chinese Herbs

Over the past fifteen years I have witnessed the powerful role that acupuncture can play in helping children develop their attention. In 1998, the National Institutes of Health published a consensus report on treatment approaches to attention deficit disorder, listing acupuncture as a promising treatment. Acupuncture, the ancient Chinese medical therapy, is based on the assumption that qi flows like streams throughout the body. By activating specific points along these streams with tiny needles, one can promote health by restoring the smooth flow of qi.

I consciously adapt my treatment approach to the specific nature of each child. While an in-depth discussion of acupuncture techniques is beyond the scope of this book, there are a few important ideas worth mentioning.

In general I begin by adjusting my own body language to the child's nature. I then work with the child's breathing in order to create a more relaxed relationship between us. In choosing points to manipulate, I use the same four-part approach described previously:

1. **Feed the Puppy Heart:** Create a secure base.

2. **Train the Puppy Heart:** Offer a secure path.

3. **Expand the Big Heart:** Offer an outlet.

4. **Develop Mastery of the Big Heart:** Enhance self-reflection.

These relationships are different for each child, and one must proceed gradually through them. Children have an exuberance of vital energy (qi). Many acupuncture practitioners do too much too fast with children. I often find that only a few points need to be used. Remember, children who are having trouble focusing are in an insecure state, making them extremely sensitive. Less is more! Never pressure a child to receive any treatment, as this proves to be counterproductive.

In many instances I begin with tuning forks or laser therapy to help accustom a child to the experience. Some children are so sensitive that these often have just as much power as the needles do. Certain children are more likely to be willing to try acupuncture than others. For example, Fire children love the novelty of sensory experience as long as it's not too intense or too stimulating. Wood children love the challenge but don't want to feel trapped. Metal children are wary of anyone invading their boundaries, so they require some time to begin to trust your intentions. Earth children may be very anxious but are afraid of upsetting you. Go gently with them. Water children are sometimes the most wary of acupuncture. Their tendency to withdraw when they're afraid can make acupuncture impossible. However, with time (and a lot of it), I have found that Water children tend to find acupuncture the most rewarding experience.

There is a double advantage to using acupuncture in treating children with ADHD. Working with the channels of qi becomes an excellent opportunity to practice directing a child's attention. I typically ask a child to focus on the point as I stimulate it. As they get better at being aware of when they get distracted, they develop greater skill at returning to focusing on the point. This is, in essence, promoting the cultivation of mindfulness.

CHINESE HERBAL MEDICINE

There are a number of excellent Chinese herbs that I find helpful in cultivating attention in children. While it's not possible to offer an in-depth discussion of herbs in this book, there are some valuable resources listed at the end of this book. Parents should always consult an experienced practitioner of Chinese herbal medicine before trying any formula.

Finding Your Spiritual Teacher

Children come into our lives to teach us something about ourselves. I always tell parents to honor this treasure. A child is a true spiritual teacher who spontaneously offers us teachings, tirelessly and for free. Where else can we find someone to show us who we are and what we, ourselves, need to work on? You don't have to go on a spiritual retreat to discover this. It's right under your nose.

While ADHD certainly puts a strain on any family, creating vicious cycles of suffering, it also presents an opportunity to rebuild relationships, find a common ground of love, share strengths, and nourish destiny. Once you recognize what your child's nature is, I encourage you to use your own creativity to discover solutions that will transform barking puppies into virtuosos. The final five chapters of this book lay out specific strategies for each of the five types of ADHD and are dedicated to those children who have discovered how to successfully tune in to this precious world. You may want to read them all or concentrate on the one that most pertains to your child's nature. May the stories in these chapters be a source of inspiration to you and your children.

Chapter 6

The Wood Child

Billy

When I first met Billy and his family he was in kindergarten and was already having trouble in school. His teacher reported that Billy couldn't sit still in class and she felt he needed something to calm him down. She was continually reprimanding him for getting out of his seat. She said she was at her wits' end and didn't know what to do with him. She had told Billy's parents to have him evaluated for ADHD.

I typically meet with parents alone at the first visit in order to discuss the developmental history freely without hurting the child's feelings. Remember, when a child is having trouble paying attention, we are dealing with an extremely insecure state. There's nothing more annoying than being forced to listen to people talk about your problems. In Billy's case, his father was unable to be there for this initial consultation. Billy's mother explained that her husband was away a lot of the time and so she would explain our meeting to him. As she talked, it was clear she was overwhelmed and worried about her son. She told me how Billy had always been a "spirited child," extremely active even in the womb. He walked at a very young age, and he was late talking, but that didn't seem to slow him down. She always had to keep a close eye on him because she'd find him climbing on something or taking off in public places. He seemed to have no sense of danger. Once, when he was four years old, Billy was found climbing on the roof of the neighbor's house, and it took all of mom's patience to stay calm and not scare him into jumping.

On the very first day of preschool, she'd received a call that Billy had run away during nap time. Like many Wood children, Billy's idea of "circle time" was running around the circle. The preschool teachers had learned to give him space to move around before activities. It was at this time that Billy became obsessed with video games, playing them for hours.

In kindergarten, Billy's behaviors became more aggressive. He would push other children whenever the kids were lining up. Billy would get in trouble during recess for fighting with other children. The principal called because Billy would blow up at the teacher, threatening her. He began attending a small social-skills group after school. By the time I saw Billy, he'd gone to the doctor several times because of recurrent headaches. His pediatrician could find nothing physically wrong and said the headaches most likely arose from stress.

In my meeting with Billy's mom, she immediately lit up when I spoke about wild puppies. "Oh, my boy's definitely a big puppy!" In order to feed the puppy, we have to know what kind of puppy we're working with. Billy's mom was quick to identity him as a Wood child: "That's him! Oh, definitely, he's a Wood boy all right." She said everyone was always saying that Billy was going to make a great lawyer someday—if he didn't end up in jail first!

After meeting Billy it was clear that he was a classic Wood child. His dark, intense eyes flicked rapidly around the room, taking everything in, and his square, muscular body moved with great speed and agility. He had to touch everything in my office, but there was a sense of urgency to his movements that revealed his insecurity. Sniffing around the office, running in and out of the rooms, and opening drawers quickly turned into pushing when his mother asked him not to touch something. It was no surprise to me that Billy became aggressive when he found his movements restricted in the classroom.

We began mapping out a solution for Billy like this:

Mapping a Solution for Wood

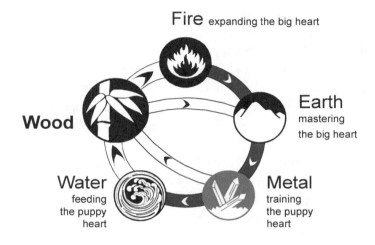

Feeding the Puppy Heart: The Nourishing Power of Water

Recognizing ADHD as a cry for help, we had to begin by creating a safe haven for Billy. This meant looking at his environment and seeing whether it was supporting his nature. Of all the children with ADHD, Wood children are perhaps the most tortured in classroom settings. This is simply not the optimal way for them to learn. Ideally, Billy would learn best by being someone's apprentice. Hands-on work is what's real to him. Building, farming, taking things apart, and anything else that involves physical interaction will feed his learning style. Humans have been learning this way for thousands of years. Unfortunately, Billy is a child of the twenty-first century and had little choice but to learn how to adapt to the physical restrictions of a modern classroom.

In creating a more secure base for Billy we needed to use Water. Water feeds Wood. What exactly does that mean? There are many metaphors for Water power in life. The most basic is drinking enough water. When a Wood child gets dry, his temperament becomes brittle and more volatile. I recommended Billy try to drink five glasses of water a day. This treatment may seem overly simple, but it has far-reaching power for the Wood child. Billy began carrying a water bottle every day to ensure that he was drinking enough water at school. Carrying a water bottle became a source of pride and security for Billy. He began to recognize the connection between his physical state and his ability to focus. It also gave him something to do, channeling his fidgetiness. While his teacher initially saw the water bottle as a potential distraction in the classroom, she discovered how such a simple intervention actually improved Billy's mood. What's more, Billy complained less about headaches.

Fish live in the water. We began Billy on daily fish oils (1000 mg DHA) and within about three weeks, his teacher began noticing a difference in his attention. He seemed less fidgety and disruptive. I find that omega-3 fatty acids are important nutrients for attention in general, and they are particularly effective for Wood children.

I suggested that Billy start swimming regularly, and his mother pointed out that when he was younger this had been one of his favorite activities. However, lately they just hadn't seemed to have the time to get into the water regularly. She recalled how calm he was when they were on vacation at the beach. Billy's love of movement was nourished by this activity, and he eventually began swimming competitively. Making a habit out of swimming gradually helped him regulate his attention. I also recommended that Billy take baths with Epsom salt each night before bed. This relaxing activity ensured he got adequate sleep, another important Water activity. When he was well rested, Billy could deal with the frustrations of the day in a less threatened way.

Bed-Wetting

It's not uncommon to find that Wood children have trouble with bed-wetting. This was a humiliating problem for Billy. Bed-wetting is a sign that the puppy brain is dominating the little-frog attentions. I asked his parents to help him develop sphincter control by having him start to urinate and then stop and then start again. Making this a positive experience became empowering for Billy, helping him discover the connection between his mind and body control.

Beware the Video Game Addiction

For Billy, as for many Wood children, one of the biggest challenges was reducing the video game addiction. Just doing this had a huge effect on his attention. Dealing with any addiction is very challenging. We had to wean him gradually and redirect him toward other activities that gave him a better sense of connection with others.

Being a Water Role Model for Your Wood Child

Creating a safe haven for Billy meant getting his parents to shape their own behavior more effectively to offer a greater sense of security. Billy's mother was very Earth natured. She was an extremely sympathetic, caring woman who often took on the role of peacemaker in her family life. She tended to worry too much about things, becoming paralyzed by Billy's behaviors and rendered unable to manage him. Billy's father, on the other hand, turned out to be very Water natured. A quiet, reserved man, he was a college professor who was away for much of the week. When we eventually met, he was at first in denial that Billy had any problem. He told me how he had always been in awe of his son's competitive nature, encouraging it in part because he himself was not naturally like that. He said he thought it would be good for Billy's survival. During our discussion he was able to recognize Billy's aggressive behavior as a call for help.

Working with Billy's father turned out to be crucial in stabilizing Billy's attention.

Water-natured people tend to deal with stress by becoming quiet rather than shouting. They don't use a lot of words. Wood children tend to focus on movement for information, and body language becomes much more important than words when the puppy heart is overstressed. In their nonverbal ways, Billy and his father had something in common that would prove useful.

All children need role models to learn how to develop their skills. Billy's dad embraced his own Water nature, learning how to use his cool detachment to recognize the early nonverbal signs that his son was getting frustrated: shoulders tightening, jaw clenching, glaring eyes. By not overreacting, he learned to calmly connect with his son in order to help Billy bring it down a notch. This meant quietly moving Billy to another setting (a walk outside, a ride in the car, a few jumping jacks) to break the cycle of "barking" before he got out of control. This kind of quiet guidance helped Billy save face and built a kind of self-confidence that allowed him time to connect his feelings to his reactions. Their relationship blossomed over the next few years.

Less Is Love

In order to be effective, Billy's father had to learn that less is more. Being too reserved, too removed, or too negative ended up frustrating Billy's Wood spirit. It simply took the wind out of Billy's sails. While just sitting and thinking was perfectly natural for Billy's father, it often felt like torture to Billy. Wood children can't handle too much "internal" work for long periods of time. Billy's father began taking him for walks in the woods on a regular basis. These outings were a great opportunity to show Billy calm attention as he and his father took turns pointing out interesting things in nature. This time together, sharing in their natures, opened up opportunities for greater intimacy, paving the way to training the puppy heart.

CULTIVATING WATER NATURE IN YOURSELF

Children teach us something about ourselves. If you don't happen to be Water natured, you can cultivate these powers in order to nourish your Wood child. Any activities that foster quiet contemplation, such as meditation or yoga, may help you better deal with your Wood child. A Wood child can turn any household upside down. When you manifest calm body language, it creates an atmosphere of safe respite for your child, reducing the need for habitual fight-or-flight behavior. But remember, this is a gradual process. The best place to begin to gain control is with yourself.

Training the Puppy Heart: The Power of Metal

Training is meant to create a secure path to channel behaviors into more productive ways to focus. Of all the relationships that I map out, Metal-Wood is perhaps the most dynamic and the most volatile. Metal prunes Wood. Without this, Wood runs wild like a weed. Billy's hyperactive movements were a sign of the need for regulation. He rushed through everything. Billy needed to learn how to slow down, but this can be extremely challenging when the Wood puppy heart feels threatened. Billy needed consistent feedback to keep him on track and connected. Metal's power lies in creating consistency through patterns and rhythms. Repetition and reward helped Billy regulate his movements through motivation. But remember, less is more. Just as too much pruning will kill a tree, too many restrictions can feel threatening. That's how Billy felt in the classroom with all those rules and regulations.

Consistency is the hallmark of Metal's power. In order to develop a sense of rhythm, Billy had to understand the flow of time. To develop this, I recommended his parents play The Time Game (see chapter 5).

In examining Billy's home life, it became clear that there was no consistency from day to day or moment to moment. Billy's parents needed to learn to give consistent signals to him. Once we were able to establish new rhythms at home, Billy actually began to feel more secure in being able to predict what was going to happen next and what was expected of him.

Mapping a Way through the Woods

I had Billy's parents create a map of his daily routine. This helped reduce his agitation and reestablished clear goals and direction for his behaviors. His mother had to learn to give nonverbal feedback rather than indulging his behaviors with promises. Wood children love having goals, and consistent feedback reinforces trust, allowing them to make connections between cause and effect, between behaviors and consequences.

Homework

The Wood child is a natural hunter, an explorer, a trailblazer, but no one likes to feel lost in the wilderness. Once Billy began first grade, that's exactly what homework felt like. We introduced The Homework Game (see chapter 5) to help him reduce frustration by giving him a sense of accomplishment. Breaking down homework assignments this way made it fun and reduced that overwhelming feeling that it was never going to end.

Metal Rhythms: The Breath

Simply expecting your child to be able to regulate his emotional state is unreasonable. This skill takes practice. Billy learned the belly-breathing technique and practiced with his dad before bed each night. Eventually, his parents found that they could ask him to do three belly breaths if they noticed the subtle signs of his frustration early enough. This helped Billy experience the feeling of shifting emotional states. The more he practiced, the better he got at redirecting his frustration.

During this period of Billy's life he started taking classes in tae kwon do, which demanded both structure (Metal) and quiet (Water). He took to it quickly and the sensei made Billy his star pupil. Experiencing his special power of movement (Wood) in a more integrated way improved Billy's sense of self-esteem. And with this boost came an increased ability to regulate his attention in group settings.

Being a Metal Role Model for Your Wood Child

His parents' creation of a consistent yet loving structure gradually helped Billy realize that he was not the center of attention. This is an important step on the path to big-heartedness.

As a parent, learning to be consistent in your own life sets the stage for much greater respect from your child. It takes practice to develop a sense for control that is natural rather than threatening. Ideally, it's best to begin very early for the Wood child, but this is not always possible.

For parents who do happen to be Metal natured, be careful. Remember, the goal is not to undermine your child's sense of security by setting too many boundaries. That can feel like a cage, which will only bring out more puppy barking. Metal-natured parents tend to judge easily, and an insecure Wood child is extremely sensitive to criticism. Be mindful of the effect you are having on your child and try to imagine what it feels like to be your Wood child. This is using your big heart. Remember, less is love.

Expanding the Big Heart: The Power of Fire

Wood gives rise to Fire. In a sense, this is Wood's destiny, its purpose: to be used as fuel to warm us and give us light, just as it's spring's destiny to become summer. Trapped in a state of insecurity, Billy had lost his sense of higher purpose as a Wood child. Unable to see the big picture, Billy could not see the effect his actions had on others. As Billy began to feel more secure in his Wood identity, we needed to find an outlet for Billy to burn off his excess energy in such a way that he could experience a broader range of emotional experiences. By directing his nature into more meaningful experiences, he could gain greater perspective on his own habitual puppy reactions.

By second grade Billy hated school and was having increasing difficulties sitting in the classroom. I suggested that he try performing in a local acting company that needed a young boy for a performance of *Peter Pan*. Performance is a great Fire activity that gave Billy an outlet for expressing himself, and he could practice focusing by memorizing lines. Billy had an amazing knack for acting and loved having the spotlight on him. More importantly, Billy began learning to be a part of an ensemble, accepting feedback and controlling his movements for the good of the performance.

Giving Voice to Wood

I suggested that Billy begin receiving private speech therapy even though his vocabulary was age appropriate. Wood children tend to rely on nonverbal (physical) expression rather than using their words. Fire corresponds to verbal expression. This gave Billy a more effective outlet for his frustration rather than the Neanderthal grunts and shouts his parents so often heard. Language has the power to regulate wild puppy behavior. The speech therapist began labeling his emotional states so that he became more aware of other options of expression open to him when he was insecure. With this came a more advanced way of exchanging ideas with others, and Billy began to feel less misunderstood.

Angry 1-2-3

Once Billy's parents began labeling his emotions they started rating the intensity (Level 1: the least, Level 3: the most). Anger is a common emotional expression for Wood children. With practice, Billy learned how to shift his anger level from 3 to 2 to 1. This was much more tangible than simply telling him to calm down. As he gradually got better at differentiating different levels of feeling within himself, he was better able to regulate his emotional impulses.

Dancing to the Beat of a Different Drummer

Billy seemed to show an interest in playing the drums, and we encouraged him initially to play along with music videos rather than just beat the drums wildly. His parents practiced calling attention to different rhythms and intensity. Learning to experience the subtle shades beyond all or nothing helps expand the big heart. Billy later was able to join a local drumming circle, which helped him establish bonds with a group of children and adults and increased his sense of belonging to something bigger than himself. Drumming has an ancient power to connect people to the "inner rhythm" that comes from cooperation and harmony. For Billy this was a great outlet for his energy. He practiced the drums before homework and found that it helped relax his body and improve his concentration.

Follow the Leader

Wood children crave leadership roles (Fire). It is their destiny. After I met with Billy's teacher, she agreed to give him a special job in the classroom that no one else was allowed to do. While not all teachers are willing to do this, for Billy it was a key to gaining trust and respect. This new responsibility and the benefits it brought had the power to keep him focused on being a part of the class rather than simply a rugged individual. Eventually this sense of connection and belonging led to a greater awareness of the needs of others (a true sign of big-heartedness) and with it, Billy became more popular.

Mastering the Big Heart: The Power of Earth

Ultimately, learning to see yourself as part of the big picture means understanding the effect you have on others. In Five Phase Dynamics, Wood invades Earth. Earth represents our common ground, the place where we meet as a group. Billy's mother, being Earth natured, was often a target for his wrath. He was constantly creating chaos in the house, fighting with his sister, yelling at his mother, and running around like a wild dog. As we worked together, she began to see how easily dominated she had been by Billy. The Metal structure gave her a framework to regain some order and calm in the home, but the real challenge was getting Billy to be more aware of the effect he was having on his family.

Mealtime was often particularly stressful for the family. Billy never wanted to stay at the table. He'd eat a few bites and then be off running. Eating is an important area for the Wood child to develop calm attention. Fast food was invented for the Wood natured. They see food as merely fuel, but traditionally mealtime was the place to meet and exchange ideas (Earth) in order to reduce stress.

You Are How You Eat

Learning to master the impulse to eat and run was very challenging for Billy. His parents had previously let him eat in front of the TV just to have some peace and quiet. This only made him more disruptive when he was at the table. I encouraged Billy to take part in the meal preparation rather than simply being served. One summer on a camping trip he began helping his mother cook meals. This seemed to open something up in him. It gave greater meaning to eating together and helped strengthen the bond with his mother. He started getting more interested in exploring different foods as well. This is always a good sign that a child is developing a greater tolerance for diversity, a big-hearted quality. Becoming more aware of different flavors made him more sensitive to different emotional states too. Recognizing that each member of his family had different preferences opened up greater empathy for the needs of others, another aspect of the big heart.

Don't Overfeed the Puppy

A major challenge in expanding Billy's diet was shifting away from the high-energy, run-for-your-life foods like sugar that simply feed the puppy heart. Carbohydrates are like kindling—they give a short burst of energy and then peter out. Billy began eating more proteins for breakfast, which helped prevent the wild blood-sugar swings that triggered much of his impulsive behavior. This diet change alone helped him develop calmer attention in class.

As a side note, be aware that stimulant medications tend to suppress the appetite. If your child is taking medications for ADHD, you may be seeing increased mood swings as his blood sugar dips. This common side effect is another reason to stick to high-protein, high-quality foods for your child.

Developing Wood Self-Reflection

It would take a few years for Billy to learn to develop mastery of his big-heartedness. This meant taking responsibility for his actions and paying closer attention to his mood shifts. Developing both retrospective awareness ("How am I today compared to yesterday?") and prospective awareness ("How will it be tomorrow compared to today?") are important exercises that helped him develop the imaginative powers that characterize neocortical function. As he began to get better at sharing his feelings, he was able to recognize the same feelings in others, too.

Meditation

Meditation is an age-old practice that helps focus the mind by bringing greater self-awareness. People often ask how I can teach meditation to a hyperactive Wood child like Billy. I have found that with the right encouragement and setting, it is actually quite easy. Telling Billy that this was a way for him to master his superpowers helped. The trick was practicing meditation at home, too. That's where parents really need to be supportive.

Wood Meditation

This meditation can be done standing, sitting, or lying down. Remember, your Wood child wants to move, so learning to be still is a challenge. Sometimes standing makes it easier at the beginning.

1. To begin, have your child do a few belly breaths: breathing in, the belly expands (not the chest); breathing out, the belly relaxes (letting go).

2. Now ask your child to imagine she is a tree, tall and strong, reaching up into the sky. While she's breathing into her belly, she should imagine the air coming into her body.*

3. As your child breathes out, have her imagine that she is letting go of her breath, giving back with kindness all her power to the earth. Let her know that the earth gives her support and allows her to grow tall and strong. The trees give back to the earth, aerating the soil with their roots.

4. As your child breathes in, guide her to silently give thanks to the air for her power. Breathing out, she'll give thanks to the earth for its support, giving back its power.

* Air is associated with the lungs and Metal in the Five Phase Correspondences. Metal trains Wood.

Wood Qigong Exercise: Standing Like a Tree

This exercise is best done outside before breakfast (facing east) to get your child going in the morning, but it's also good to try before doing homework. By doing these exercises with your child you'll make them feel less like another chore.

1. Have your child stand with her legs separated, shoulder-width apart, feet flat on the ground. Ask her to imagine that she is a tree with a broad trunk.

2. As she faces forward, ask her to look at nothing in particular, just letting her gaze wander without attaching to anything.

3. Now have her hold her hands in front of her at the level of her belly button as if she were wrapping her arms around a beach ball.

4. As she breathes into her belly (see basic belly-breathing exercise in chapter 5) allow the beach ball to expand slightly. As she breathes in, have her imagine that she is so filled with air that she's able to bend in the wind. Light as air, ask her to try smiling.

5. As she releases her breath, ask her to allow the beach ball to deflate slightly. At the same time, have her relax her posture slightly and feel her weight go down to the bottom of her feet. She can imagine that these are her roots, keeping her grounded.

6. Start with one or two breaths and work with her over the weeks to increase the number of breaths to twenty-five. As she practices, ask her to try to focus only on her posture and the movement of her breath.

Chanting with the Wood Child: Chanting is a great adjunct to try after meditating. Chanting is essentially repeating a word or a short series of sounds over and over. I often use, "Okay, okay, okay, okay. . . ." Have your child notice how the sound of the words changes as she relaxes and focuses with greater flexibility.

Expanding Compassion

Being able to see things from another's perspective is the true power of the big heart. As Billy developed a sense of greater security in who he was, he began noticing when his mother was sad and would spontaneously settle down. In working with Billy, I mapped out how Wood disrupts Earth. This helped him gain greater self-reflection. He would tell his mother when he thought he needed to see me for a "tune-up," as he called them. During these sessions we would first do acupuncture and then a short meditation to practice imagining feeling another's emotions.

Storytelling is a great way to practice this. We made little comic books in which an imagined child with Earth qualities was being bullied. Then we came up with various emotions that that child might feel. Moving beyond the black and white of good guy/bad guy allowed Billy to begin exploring a range of emotions through the characters.

Trading-Places Exercises

We also began role-playing with Billy. I suggested that he and his father set up a game in which they got to trade places for an hour: Billy would be the dad and his father would be the child. This enhanced Billy's ability to see through another's eyes.

Cultivating Earth Qualities

Ultimately Billy had to discover that he needed a social group as much as they needed him. This is the power of love that makes us feel whole, freeing us from the bonds of insecurity and barking puppies. It wasn't until Billy spent a summer away from home that he began to truly appreciate the special qualities of his family, a sign that he was internalizing Earth qualities. This is how he moved from embracing individualism to community.

Embracing Diversity: Becoming a True Hero for the World

Below are some activities parents, teachers, and therapists can work into homework assignments to help develop the Wood child's strengths:

- Come up with three examples of things that you can do better by working with others than by working alone.

- Explain the meaning of "cooperation," "hero," and "sacrifice."

- Describe something that you do better with the family than alone.

- Work with the rest of the class to solve a problem.

- Defining community: illustrate or list as many members of your community as you can.

- Describe characteristics of a friend in detail (what nature are they?).

- Come up with games that exhibit cooperation to play with a friend.

- Teach a game that requires teamwork to family members.

- Explain the meaning of "humanitarian."

- Read a biography of a famous humanitarian (or more than one).

Teaching the Wood Child

Teachers certainly play an important role in any child's development. However, because they're under such pressure to conform to curricula these days, they usually don't have the time to attend to individual needs. A teacher who can use the right mix of Metal (consistency) and Water (calm quiet) will promote the kind of optimum stress that gets a Wood child like Billy to meet challenges without feeling threatened. Wood-natured teachers may have compassion for like-minded children, but this can sometimes lead to conflict when the child questions their authority. Fire-natured teachers are excellent sources of inspiration for the Wood child, offering excitement and change to keep her focused. Earth-natured teachers' main focus is often on group activities and the Wood child may be tempted to dominate the group. It's important that there is enough Metal consistency to support the group in such settings.

Regardless of the nature of the teacher, it's important to remember that the Wood child who is hyperactive reflects a threatened state. Creating a supportive environment that nurtures her curiosity while teaching her skills that regulate her behaviors (expanding her big heart) will have a life-changing influence on her future academic successes. When the Wood child is tuned in to the class, she can be a real leader whose enthusiasm for doing well can focus the whole group.

Billy Tuned In

When Billy first came to me he was hostile and hyperactive. He and his parents managed to turn his problem into his advantage. He's now in fifth grade and is able to focus in class without feeling threatened by the demands of his teachers. He has developed some solid friendships that reinforce qualities like cooperation and trust, reducing self-centered behaviors. Starting school each fall still feels like punishment for him, but there are enough rewards for doing well in school built into his daily routine that the ups and downs of frustration have lessened as he has matured. He recently joined the Boy Scouts, and his energy and creativity have made him a great role model for the younger boys, especially on weekend camping trips. His mother told me that she now looks forward to his return after these adventures because he is so appreciative of being home. His improved self-esteem has reduced the animosity at home and each time he returns, these effects seem to last a little longer. Billy has also found success as a competitive swimmer and his once-distant father tries never to miss his swim meets.

Though it might be tempting to think that Wood kids are mainly boys, here's a story about a Wood teenager with ADHD who found a way to reduce her medications using mapping and acupuncture.

• *Rachel: A Wood Teenager with ADHD*

Rachel was fifteen years old when she first came for evaluation. She was angry at being there and responded in short grunts, claiming that she hated her parents and that no doctors could help her. She'd been treated with a series of stimulant medications for ADHD over the years, each seeming to lose its effectiveness within a few months. When I first saw her, Rachel was on a cocktail of stimulants and anti-anxiety drugs. She had been thrown out of several schools because of her hostile behavior. She blamed everyone else for her problems and had developed no close friendships. She did have a boyfriend, but he was a couple of years older than her and had had a drug problem. Her psychiatrist had suggested that Rachel consider seeing me for acupuncture.

At our second meeting, I explored Rachel's Wood nature with her. This was the first time someone had redefined her problem as an exaggerated reflection of her natural abilities. In mapping out her relationships, she was also able to identify her parents' natures: her father as Fire natured and her mother as a mix of Metal and Earth. Her parents tended to fight quite often and they were also frequently in conflcit with Rachel. Her father would often unpredictably blow up at her, while her mother was always judging her and placing harsh restrictions on Rachel's activities. As we mapped this out, Rachel was able to gain a new perspective on her life. There rose a glimmer of hope that we might develop a good therapeutic bond.

I suggested she receive some acupuncture to help relieve her tension. I often find that Wood children need concrete bodywork rather than abstract talking to ground them before probing deeper into old behavior patterns. I explained to Rachel that we could use the same relationships among the five phases to choose acupuncture points on her body. She was intrigued and wanted to know the purpose of each point. By focusing her attention on the meaning of the points, she gained greater confidence and insight into tangible ways of helping herself. She began taking DHA omega-3 fatty acids, Chinese herbs to support the kidney (Water) and balance the liver (Wood), and supplements to help with adrenal stress. This supplementation included taurine, 5-htp (an amino-acid supplement that helps with anxiety), magnesium, B_6, l-theanine, and niacin. During her acupuncture sessions, I taught Rachel how to focus her mind on the points while breathing and encouraged her to practice this each night before bed. Gradually, she began to pay closer attention to her emotional shifts and started using her breathing in situations in which she felt out of control. This was particularly helpful when her parents were arguing. Making a connection between her feelings and her reactions enabled her to appreciate other people's emotional states without just reacting, and she began talking more about the people in her life. Being able to describe her feelings in greater detail enabled her to regulate the intensity of her emotional states. Over time we were able to wean her off much of her medications, though she remained on a small dose of Adderall to help her in school. Her appetite and sleep gradually improved, creating the opportunity for a more stable and balanced quality of attention. Perhaps most importantly, we were able to develop a trusting relationship over the next few years that gave her space to express her feelings rather than simply reacting. She has become a wonderful musician and is now finishing her third year in college. Her relationship with her mom and dad has matured over the years. Rachel is now able to see them in a new light, appreciating their genuine pride in her accomplishments.

Cultivating Compassion for Wood

When the Wood child finds her big heart, she has all the virtues of a real hero: the ability to meet challenges with kindness and a willingness to sacrifice herself for others. These are characteristics of some of our most beloved leaders. Keep these in mind as your pave a path for your Wood child. Watch how high you set your expectations. Remember how sensitive your child's pride is. Be aware of the tone of your voice. Is it accusatory or encouraging? Is it calm or shrill and demeaning? Remember that your words can feel like swords if they are too sharp, too critical. Try imagining what it feels like to be her in your presence. Are you consistent in the limits you set? Do you follow through with your promises? Are you creating structure without being rigid or mean? Are you indulging her puppy heart just because it's easier? In order to open her big heart, you need to see the big picture too. If you make this your daily practice you become just the right medicine for your child.

Please remember these qualities in dealing with the intense energy of the Wood child, whether she's in your home or your classroom. She's here to teach us all something about ourselves. The virtues of Wood lie in the power to be in the zone, to keeps things moving forward. Wood feeds Fire's expressions of joy and delight. Wood gives Water an outlet into the world. Wood gives Earth direction. And Wood gives Metal something to shape. Loving Wood is loving all the life that spring brings forth in our world.

A Summary of the Approach to Wood

- **Feeding the Puppy Heart:** Use Water to nourish. Give fish oils; increase fluids; prioritize bathing, other water-based activities (like swimming), and sleep. Work on timing and cultivate mystery. Try craniosacral therapy and acupuncture.

- **Training the Puppy Heart:** Metal regulates, so support structure, explore patterns, and maintain consistency. Work with breathing rhythm, martial arts, and mapping.

- **Expanding the Big Heart:** Fire serves as an outlet. Encourage performance and leadership. Consider speech therapy, dance, and gymnastics.

- **Mastering the Big Heart:** Recognize how Wood invades Earth. Practice eating together, playing I Spy, and chanting/singing together. Use The Breathing Exercise and activities that help embrace diversity (becoming a true hero).

Chapter 7

The Fire Child

Lizzie

Lizzie is such a character! With her sparkling eyes, big rosy cheeks, and bright smile, she lights up the room with her excitement. Everyone who meets her enjoys being around her. When Lizzie was in the second grade, her parents contacted me because they were told she was having trouble focusing in class. The teacher said Lizzie needed to get more serious about her work or else she wouldn't move to the next grade. Lizzie had become very distracted by anything going on in the classroom. Even the tags on her shirt seemed to bother her in class. She began complaining that it was too loud in the class, and this was worse whenever the class had to be really serious. Her mom was aware that Lizzie was immature for her age and Lizzie's impulse control was certainly not as good as that of the other kids in her class. By the middle of the year she had even begun talking in baby talk.

When I contacted Lizzie's teacher she told me that Lizzie was very popular and added liveliness to her classroom, but she complained that Lizzie didn't know when to stop being silly. She'd become a bit of a class clown. The teacher clearly loved Lizzie, but she was concerned that the work in third grade was going to be much harder and that Lizzie would have a lot of trouble surviving it.

When I first spoke to Lizzie's parents, it quickly became obvious that Lizzie was a Fire child. There's never a dull moment when you have a Fire child in your home. I find that it's often easy to pick them out in a crowd. The intensity and abundance of their spirit can be felt from the moment they're born. Lizzie had a natural sense of humor and was highly intuitive. Her ability to sense when something was going to happen sometimes made her anxious. Lizzie was caught between two extremes: she would be intensely attracted to stimulation but easily overwhelmed by it. That's a sign that her puppy heart was dominating her attention. Lizzie told me that school was boring. In fact, her mother said that Lizzie complained that *everything* was boring. This, too, is a classic sign of insecurity. In our first meeting, Lizzie's parents and I mapped out a way to expand her attention.

Mapping a Solution for Fire

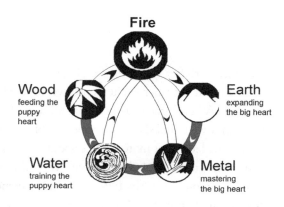

Feeding the Puppy Heart: The Power of Wood

In nature, wood is the fuel for fire. For Lizzie, that meant having someone whose encouragement would inspire her to feel safe. Luckily, Lizzie's father had just the right Wood nature to get her going. However, he needed to learn how to use his power wisely. Feeding the puppy heart means creating a secure base without simply indulging it. The Fire child loves stimulation to the point of losing control. This is where the power of less is love is really important. Too much push from Wood makes Fire burn out of control. Lizzie's father began to see how his own drive to succeed was making Lizzie feel more insecure, amplifying her Fire nature. He recognized that shouting had the same effect. When Lizzie felt insecure, she was easily startled, creating a kind of vicious cycle in which distraction created more excitement.

Lizzie's father had overstimulated her as a baby because she seemed to like it so much. As this became a habit, Lizzie never experienced calm attention. Her mother, a Metal-natured lawyer, had been less encouraging in an effort to balance her husband. Over time she became too rigid in her expectations of Lizzie. Lizzie had been put in far too many after-school activities and had no downtime. Her parents complained that they'd find her on the computer in the middle of the night.

In redefining Lizzie's sense of security, the first thing we did was reduce all the entertainment and push less. Less is love. But that doesn't mean eliminating everything. That's too cruel for a Fire child. Gentle encouragement goes a long way. Setting clear goals that are attainable and not just giving in to instant gratification is the key to developing proper Wood nourishment for the Fire child. These limits actually reduced Lizzie's anxiety and improved her focus.

Creating a stronger sense of security meant meeting Lizzie where she was. Because she loved novelty, we began mapping out her day. This gave her something to look forward to and reduced her anxiety by orienting her to what was happening in sequence. Preparing her for transitions during her day made her less likely to become overwhelmed by sudden changes.

Getting more exercise also had a big effect on Lizzie's attention. Remember, Wood is physical movement. Simply going for a walk after school helped her settle down before she did her homework. I also recommended that Lizzie be allowed to get up from doing her homework for a few minutes at regular intervals to keep it from getting too "boring." Lizzie and her mom started doing yoga together and found it to be a great way to reduce Lizzie's sensory overload at the end of the day.

Interestingly, I often find that children with Fire-type ADHD symptoms in elementary school sometimes improve once they get to middle school, where they're allowed to change classes. The change of scenery refreshes their attention and keeps them grounded.

Wood Nourishing Diet

Lizzie's dramatic mood swings were often linked to bouts of low blood sugar. The Fire child's metabolism burns very hot. When she gets hungry she's liable to crash quickly. That's when it becomes impossible to focus on anything but food. Lizzie would get wildly dramatic, become giddy, or simply fall asleep. Through our work, her parents learned to recognize these as warning signs of low blood sugar. By reducing her carbohydrate load, increasing proteins, and increasing the number of meals from three to five per day, we were able to stabilize her mood. Fire children tend to seek comfort in food as a reward. It's important to remember that restricting sweets when they are in the house never works. It only makes your Fire child focus more on getting them. Although Lizzie's parents were vegetarians, they realized the powerful effect meat had on stabilizing their daughter's mood and sense of security.

Training the Puppy Heart: The Power of Water

Lizzie's bright red cheeks, frequent sweating, and sensitivity to noise and textures were signs of a heightened state of insecurity. She was burning too hot and needed cooling down. Training the puppy heart means offering a secure path for her nature through repetition and reward. Water cools Fire. We began by making sure Lizzie drank adequate fluids all day. She'd often get so caught up in what she was doing that she'd simply forget to drink. Just drinking more water (not sweetened beverages) lessened her hypersensitivities to textures by reducing her internal heat. Reducing excessive sweet foods in favor of some salty foods (salt is the flavor of Water in Chinese medicine) helped regulate the intense cravings Lizzie had. We added omega-3 fish oils (500 mg a day) to her diet as well. Remember, an engine that is burning too hot needs oil to ensure smooth function and needs water in the radiator to prevent overheating.

Water Massage and Sleep

Lizzie's love of sensory stimulation made it difficult for her to settle down and make the transition to sleep. She was afraid of the dark and didn't really know how to fall asleep. Typically, she would just play until she dropped. Water corresponds to the dead of night. It can mean the end of fun (and light) for the Fire child. Respecting this challenge, I recommended her parents give her Epsom salt baths and deep massage before bed. This became a great way for her to unwind and bond with her parents. Her parents also got her a wave machine and a night-light to put in her room to help her feel more secure and direct her into sleep. Getting enough sleep helped restore her parasympathetic-sympathetic nervous-system balance and Lizzie found it much easier to deal with stimulation the following day.

Being a Water Role Model for Your Fire Child

In a sense, the job of Water is to settle down and be serious. Water is deep and quiet and still. This is perhaps the biggest challenge a Fire child faces. Lizzie's parents had to learn how to become calmer and quieter to counterbalance her energy when she got wild. Remember, the puppy heart reads body language before words. Lizzie's dad found that the quieter he got, the more she could settle down and focus. They made a habit of having some quiet reading time together every day. Lizzie fell in love with the adventures of Harry Potter. Unlike TV or video games, reading has a slower, more organic pace of processing that helps train attention. Removing the computer from Lizzie's room was another important step in helping her sleep better, although at first it felt like punishment to her. Actually, Lizzie told me she was sometimes so sensitive that she could feel that there was a computer in a room even when it was off.

Less Is Love

While Water certainly has the power to regulate Fire, please be cautious. Too much water can put the fire out. Being too "Watery" (too aloof, too detached) can cause your Fire child to become more insecure. Demanding her to "be serious" can be terribly threatening if it's done all the time. If you happen to be a Water-natured parent, be mindful of the power you have over your child. Sometimes all you need to do to keep her on track is just sit by her side saying nothing while she's doing her homework.

Training the puppy heart means offering positive rewards. Don't forget to honor your child's temperament. Don't take your child's behaviors personally. Your child may mistake your Water nature as an indication that you're too busy for her. Remember that the Fire child has her senses open wide. Be aware that too much silence may be undermining her feeling of security. Listen to your tone of voice: Is it aloof or inspiring? Recognizing her tendency toward drama, you can catch these mood shifts early with just a little gentle grounding. Getting your Fire child used to being alone takes time and practice. Be patient and supportive. Ultimately, when you can regulate your own nature, you become a role model who strengthens your Fire child's ability to stay calm and focused in places like the classroom, too.

Calming the Environment

Lizzie's parents made subtle changes in her environment to help promote calm. They painted the ceiling of her bedroom blue and put tiny white stars and a yellow moon on it that glowed in the dark. She loved this and it gave her comfort each night when she went to sleep.

Burning in Homework Hell

Doing homework with Lizzie was one of the biggest challenges. She'd come home from school and have huge meltdowns. Giving her a protein snack and free time to play first made it easier for her to reengage in work. Her parents found that she did better by intermittently changing where she worked. Because Lizzie had been diagnosed with ADHD she was able to receive accommodations through Section 504 of the Americans with Disabilities Act, allowing her less homework in the first years of school. In the long run, having less homework actually allows some Fire children more time to recharge in order to be more attentive the next day.

Expanding the Big Heart: The Power of Earth

Just as fruit ripens at the end of summer, Fire gives birth to Earth. Earth represents context, relationships, and connections. Living in the moment, Lizzie tended to forget what she learned by the next day. We found that she was able to retain information much better when she understood how things were related. For example, when she was learning geography, if Lizzie connected the information about places to characters she knew, it was much easier for her to remember information about the place. By adding information she learned each day to a big sheet of paper and connecting it all by strings, she was better able to see how everything fit into the big picture. This is learning by context, an Earth action.

Lizzie seemed to just know things through her feelings. When too much information was coming in, she would get overwhelmed. We began teaching Lizzie how to see the connections between bits of information. Practicing analogies helped. Children in first and second grade are able to understand simple analogies (for instance, a fish is to water as a bird is to . . .). As a child gets older, these can be expanded into more complex relationships. (See the resources for books on analogy.) For Lizzie, understanding relationships helped her see beyond the all-or-nothing perspective.

Flash Cards

Lizzie also discovered the power of flash cards. Many children use these, but somehow I find that Fire children really do well with this learning aid. Lizzie found that just making flash cards was annoying, so her mother tried to make it fun by using different colors, shapes, and stickers. It became a great way for Lizzie to organize all the material she had to learn. Lizzie would lay out the cards to help her understand the different ways the information fit together. Her parents quizzed her by using the same cards, and this practice showed exactly what Lizzie knew and what she still needed to work on without getting totally overwhelmed by *everything*. This gave her the broader view that is the key to expanding the big heart for the Fire child.

Speech Therapy

Being impulsive, Lizzie had trouble getting her thoughts out fast enough. This contributed to her frustration. A good speech therapist can offer the kind of one-to-one exercises that help the Fire child use her words instead of simply reacting. Lizzie's parents also began labeling her emotional states as they arose, much like one would label colors. Gradually, Lizzie learned to describe what she was feeling rather than simply overreacting. Such language abilities are an example of how the big heart calms the drama of the puppy heart.

Cooking

Getting Lizzie to cook was a wonderful way for her to discover the shades of sensory experience. Cooking is like magic, transforming one thing into something else. Exploring the diversity of textures, flavors, and smells helped open Lizzie up to focusing on more subtle experiences. Lizzie began watching cooking shows on TV and became quite proud of the creations she made for dinner. This activity had the added reward of doing things for others. Lizzie still loves to cook; in fact, she recently told me that she intends to become a famous chef one day.

"Row, Row, Row Your Boat"

Lizzie had a wonderful singing voice. I encouraged her to sing with others in order to experience the power of sharing. The give-and-take of harmonizing reduces self-centered attention and it allowed Lizzie to develop control over the rhythm of her breath and the volume of her voice. You and your Fire child can try practicing songs in a round, like "Row, Row, Row Your Boat." This helps your child pay attention to what he's doing amidst the other voices. With practice, your child will find it easier to focus as he moves "gently down the stream."

Becoming a Mentor

The destiny of Fire is to become Earth. Expanding the big heart means opening up a path to one's destiny. For Lizzie, this meant learning that the world did not revolve around her. When Lizzie's third-grade teacher gave her a chance to tutor the kindergarten kids, Lizzie loved it. Spending time with younger children helped her gain a new perspective on her own emotional immaturity. Initially drawn to the younger children because they weren't so serious, she gradually felt the responsibility of being in a mentoring position and took it very seriously. In fact, when Lizzie got older she was even able to make a job out of tutoring. This was great for her self-esteem and it prompted her to stay organized in order to be helpful to others. This experience would go a long way in helping Lizzie discover her natural role as a leader. By the time she got to high school she had become the head of her student council, laying the groundwork for truly mastering her Fire power.

Mastering the Big Heart: The Power of Metal

Lizzie initially had been very disruptive in her classroom. This was certainly not intentional. Rules and regulations (Metal structure) didn't seem to matter to her when she was feeling something intensely (Fire can melt Metal). In fact, the disruption was Lizzie's way of breaking up monotony by trying to experience things in a new way. Unfortunately this is a great source of conflict and confusion in school settings. The pressure to stay on track with the curriculum is simply too great these days, and Fire children get in big trouble for having too much fun. For Lizzie to really develop mastery of her big heart, she had to become more aware of the effect she was having on her surroundings. This meant understanding how Fire melts Metal.

Mapping the Day

For Lizzie, creating a map of her day that began when she woke up and ended with bedtime enabled her to appreciate the order and sequence of activities without getting overwhelmed and panicking. Her teacher adopted the same strategy in school, mapping out class activities for the next day with Lizzie. This helped Lizzie focus on the big picture and remain calm. Initially, Lizzie needed plenty of coaching to remind her to use her map but it eventually became second nature.

Fire Meditation

Breathing is one of the simplest ways to cultivate Metal in Fire. Once Lizzie learned and began to use some simple breathing exercises, she was able to directly experience the emotional shifts in her body. There is comfort in this kind of rhythm, and Lizzie became comfortable and secure enough to gradually experience a range of emotional states rather than just excitement. This kind of mastery of Fire can only come with lots of practice. Here is a typical meditation I use with some Fire children. This meditation can be done sitting or lying down, in a dimly lit room (best with a single candle).

1. To begin, do a few belly breaths. Breathing in, the belly expands (not the chest); breathing out, the belly relaxes (letting go).

2. Now ask your child to imagine that he is a candle in a dark room. As he breathes in to his belly, have him imagine the air in the room feeding his flame.

3. As he breathes out, he can imagine that he's letting go of his light, filling the whole room. Ask him to try to be a steady candle, undisturbed by the breathing in or out. He can let his breath come in and out softly and slowly.

4. As he breathes in, have him silently give thanks to the air that feeds his flame. Breathing out, have him give thanks to the room that keeps his flame safe from being blown out.

Fire Qigong Exercise: Standing Like the Sun

This exercise is best done at noon, before lunch, and facing south, but it can be practiced anytime. You might want to try it with your child in the morning, before he goes to school.

1. Have your child stand with legs separated, shoulder-width apart, feet flat on the ground. Ask him to imagine that he is the sun.

2. As he faces straight forward, ask him to allow his gaze to focus on nothing in particular.

3. He'll start his with hands down at his sides. As he breathes in to his belly (see basic belly-breathing exercise in chapter 5), have him slowly raise his arms up and out, like sunrays. He'll move them up and over his head and clasp his hands. Then ask him to turn his still-clasped hands up, palms to the sky.

4. Guide him to take a big breath in and look up at the back of his hands clasped, as if he were holding the sun. As he holds the breath, ask him to try smiling.

5. Have your child release his breath slowly and allow his arms to retrace their path out and back down to his sides.

6. Start with one or two breaths and have him work his way up to twenty-five over the weeks. As you practice together, ask him to try to focus only on his posture and the movement of his breath.

Heart-Rate Coherence and Acupuncture

Lizzie needed to internalize the powers of Metal to create order. I began by teaching her how to regulate her heart rhythm (Fire) and breath (Metal) using an emWave device in my office (see resources). The emWave is designed to bring about heart-lung coherence, and this has been shown to improve attention and reduce excess stress responses. Lizzie's parents eventually bought a portable emWave that she used at home before bedtime. In my own practice I've found that using the emWave in conjunction with acupuncture is particularly effective for Fire children, as it helps them experience the calming effect that comes with focusing on specific acupuncture points. Lizzie enjoyed coming for acupuncture, in part because she loved sensation so much. Very few acupuncture points needed to be stimulated to bring her to a state of calm focus. We could then use the acupuncture sessions to practice becoming aware of the way her emotions shifted from moment to moment. She found that the more experience she had with calm attention, the better she was able to regulate her emotional states in the classroom.

Flower Essences and Aromatherapy

Flowers and plants can be very helpful to your child. Flower essences and aromatherapy support the Metal-Fire relationship, and I find them particularly useful for the highly sensitive Fire child. Lizzie's parents recognized how certain scents affected her mood. Metal is associated with the lungs, which are said to open at the nose. Over the years we have experimented with different essential oils in her room and on her clothes to help her awareness remain calm and open. (See appendix for more guidance on plant-based help for Fire.)

Expanding Compassion

Lizzie became very proud of her Fire nature, and she loved learning how to develop the powers of her big heart. One aspect of this power meant being able to gain a broader view of how her emotions changed from day to day. Reviewing her feelings from one day to the next helped her predict how she might feel the following day. Making a connection between her emotional states and her environment, Lizzie began to understand whom she was most likely to annoy (Metal) when she got out of control. With greater self-awareness, she was gradually able to modulate the intensity of her emotional reactions. With greater confidence, she could smile when her parents said, "Lizzie, you're using a little too much Fire right now."

Red Light, Green Light, 1-2-3

One of the simplest games we played to develop impulse control was Red Light, Green Light, 1-2-3. Lizzie would run toward me as I counted and then have to freeze when I got to three. She loved learning to control her exuberance (Fire) while staying focused on the rules (Metal). As Lizzie got older, playing board games with other kids also helped her respect the calm that comes with order. The positive feedback she got from having fun without losing control helped her develop greater tolerance for other children's behavior.

Embracing Diversity: Becoming a True Leader of the World

Below are some activities parents, teachers, and therapists can work into homework assignments to help develop the Fire child's strengths:

- Create a collage that describes your life.

- Explain the meaning of "symmetry," "pattern," and "sequence."

- Explain the meaning of "sacred" and "holy."

- Come up with three examples of ceremonies in your family.

- Describe the details of one ceremony in your family.

- Develop one daily ritual in your life.

- Come up with a way to bring something sacred into your daily life.

- Many spiritual traditions teach that we can light a candle for someone as a way to remember them or send them a blessing. You can explain your take on this ceremony and light a candle for someone before bed.

- Read biographies of famous artists or scientists.

Teaching the Fire Child

Finding the right teacher for the Fire child is very important, especially in the early years of school when attitudes about learning are being formed. A teacher who is too stimulating (too much Wood) may create more drama. When a Fire child feels secure in a classroom his enthusiasm is often a great asset to the class. Because the Fire child is so sensitive, any teacher who is feeling overly stressed (as is common today) can unknowingly trigger his wild puppy-heart impulses. Each year I would meet with Lizzie's parents to discuss options for teachers in the coming year. One year, a teacher gave each child nicknames and Lizzie's was "Baby." While the teacher thought this would be a way to get Lizzie to grow up, it actually had the opposite effect, causing her to act more like a baby. Finding a balance between Water (quiet, calm) and Wood (encouraging, goal driven) in a teacher isn't always possible. A Wood-natured teacher who can generate the right kind of direction will keep the Fire child moving toward goals. An Earth-natured teacher who encourages cohesiveness in the classroom rather than divisiveness can go a long way in developing the Fire child. If a Metal-natured teacher can stand the heat (silliness), she may actually create a perfect haven of security through her consistency. Ultimately, what matters is finding a teacher who will appreciate your Fire child's natural joy of life, his enthusiasm and high engagement with whatever is happening. A teacher who can harness this energy can help your child become a real asset for any classroom.

Lizzie Tuned In

Lizzie has done remarkably well over the years. Elementary school was rough, but by the time she got to middle school she had settled down and learned to regulate her emotional states more effectively. She has been coming to me for acupuncture and meditation practices for many years. Her mother saw the benefits of regular visits and worked hard not to miss appointments. Now in high school, Lizzie has become a natural star of the softball team, which has been great for her self-esteem. Lizzie joins her mom in classes at a local yoga studio, which has been great for their relationship. She's learned how to master her charisma effectively in school. She is a kindhearted young woman who is planning to go to college to become a teacher. I bet she'll be the most popular teacher in any school that's lucky enough to have her.

Now let's look at the story of a Fire teenager who learned how to become a healer.

• *Brandon: A Fire Teenager with ADHD*

Brandon first came to me when he was thirteen years old, at the peak of hormonal changes. He'd always had a high sense of drama in his life, but now things seemed to be falling apart. His impulse control was getting worse rather than better as he got older. He'd been suspended after he was caught stealing papers from the teacher's desk, apparently on a dare from some of the other students. He was doing poorly in school and complained that everything was boring. Brandon's parents were considering moving him to a different school, which Brandon strongly objected to. He didn't want to leave the friends he loved so much. He had been diagnosed with ADHD and placed on a stimulant medication, but by the time I first saw him, I could tell that the drugs were not helping. If anything, they were worsening the situation. While Brandon did get his work done, he couldn't retain anything, and he began having panic attacks. His personality became uncharacteristically morose, and he found it impossible to fall asleep even when the medications were at the lowest doses. Before switching him to another medication regimen, his parents consulted me.

Brandon was much quicker than his parents in recognizing his Fire nature when we met. In working with him, at first it was challenging to get him to settle down. His fast talking and wisecracking were signs of his insecurity. Shifting my own body language helped Brandon to feel calmer, and he began to be able to relax. In fact, he began to look forward to these visits. He called them his "cool-out" sessions, and he was able to tell his mother when he needed to come for a visit (evidence of his growing self-awareness). During acupuncture, I introduced him to some breathing exercises coupled with a visualization in which he imagined that he was sitting at the bottom of the sea. The ripples above were his changing breath, his sensations, and passing thoughts, but the power of his focus came from remaining calm.

He found that taking DHA omega-3 fish oils, magnesium glycinate, and 5-htp (an amino-acid supplement that helps with anxiety), along with some gentle Chinese herbs, dramatically reduced his impulsivity (see appendix).

Brandon's life was very chaotic. His parents worked long hours and there was little consistency at home. I found that working with his parents was just as important as my sessions with him. Getting them to develop routines, particularly with regard to eating regularly, was the biggest challenge. In fact, as Brandon learned to recognize his own Fire nature, he recognized the benefit of routines for the whole family. However, it wasn't until Brandon's father had a heart attack that everything seemed to change. It was a wake-up call for the whole family, especially Brandon. Suddenly, priorities shifted. Rather than just panicking, Brandon began taking his health seriously, including getting enough sleep and eating better. This health maintenance helped his grades improve. His focus became clearer, and though he has found it easier to be serious when he needs to, he has also found a way to use his wonderful sense of humor to relieve stress in others. He's been taking more responsibility around the house and has actually become a role model for his Wood-natured father, whom he has taught to meditate in order to slow down and smell the roses. Brandon is now in his first year of college and is thinking about becoming an acupuncturist.

A Summary of the Approach to Fire

- **Feeding the Puppy Heart:** Use Wood strategies, including increasing movement, mapping out the day, and providing steady fuel with a protein breakfast.

- **Training the Puppy Heart:** Water strategies include focusing on better sleep, using games to sharpen memory, and using fish oils, more water, and salty rather than sweet foods.

- **Expanding the Big Heart:** Use Earth to provide an outlet, including cooking, blood-sugar control, singing, mentoring, practicing analogies, using flash cards, and speech therapy.

- **Mastering the Big Heart:** Metal activities help regulate, including Fire qigong; breathing meditation; emWave; aromatherapy; Red Light, Green Light, 1-2-3; and activities that help embrace diversity.

Chapter 8

The Earth Child

Alex

Alex is a sweet boy with big lips and a rather shy disposition. He came to see me for an ADHD evaluation when he was in the sixth grade. His parents told me that it was only recently, when Alex entered middle school, that they realized he was having problems. They'd been told at a recent meeting with teachers that Alex was very disorganized and seemed to be falling behind in all his assignments. Looking back, they realized that his grades had been slowly dropping over the last few years. They were told that Alex wasn't living up to his potential, that he seemed to be lost in class. When Alex was called on, his answers often had nothing to do with the question. Alex had recently begun going to the nurse's office complaining of stomachaches. His pediatrician found nothing wrong but put him on antacids to see if that helped.

At home, Alex's biggest problem was making decisions. Even picking out what to wear in the morning had become difficult. His mother told me that he'd become very clingy and she often found him quietly crying in his room at night. When asked why, he said he didn't know. His older brother had been teasing him about being a wimp. When I asked about friends, Alex's mom told me that Alex worried that he wasn't going to be included in their activities. Alex had been devastated when he wasn't chosen for a Little League team the preceding summer. Since then, he'd stopped doing any sports and begun to gain weight.

Alex's mother felt that the workload at school was just too hard for Alex. His procrastination often kept him up past midnight, doing homework. Alex's mom told me: "It's like he's working, but nothing gets done." When I began seeing him, Alex had begun spending a lot of time on Facebook, checking what his classmates were doing instead of doing his work.

When I spoke with Alex it took him a long time to warm up. He sat slumped in his chair, gazing at the floor. Early on, I asked him to draw a picture of his family for me. Looking around the room and seeing drawings from other children, he initially said he couldn't draw. But some gentle encouragement helped him show that he drew quite well, and I told him so. He began each response to my questions with a tentative "I don't know," and he required coaxing to answer more fully. Eventually he told me that he liked school but thought it was too hard. When I asked about his sleeping habits, he told me that he'd been having trouble falling asleep lately because he couldn't stop his mind from thinking. When I asked what he was thinking about, he first told me that he was worried about his father. When asked why, Alex admitted that he was afraid something was going to happen to his dad. Eventually he let me know about other things he worried about. He was upset because he wasn't invited to one of the popular kids' birthday parties. As he loosened up, his stories began meandering. He couldn't seem to get to the point.

In our first interview it took a while for Alex's parents to identify him as an Earth child. His caring and natural affinity for understanding the needs of others actually gave them some relief. Terms like "pleaser" and "peacemaker" resonated with them immediately. Alex also had trouble making up his mind about his nature. He said he had a little bit of all five. This is very common. Earth children are like chameleons. They often take on characteristics of those around them in an effort to fit in. We then mapped out a solution to Alex's attention problems.

Mapping a Solution for Earth

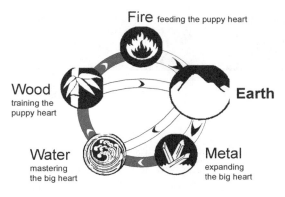

Feeding the Puppy Heart: The Power of Fire

Feeding the puppy heart meant finding a way to help Alex feel more secure. The first thing I needed to do was to lighten up the mood when I spoke with him. Fire feeds Earth, and humor is an excellent Fire way to loosen the burden that comes with too much thinking. Taking a playful approach is one of the easiest ways to engage the Earth child and develop trust. Because Earth children want to please, we set up a game in which we took turns adding elements to a figure, which helped get and keep our connection going. By doing something silly, like drawing a head with five eyes, I showed Alex that his visits with me weren't going to be like other doctor visits. His mood visibly lightened, and he began opening up. He began to speak about more personal things. For example, he let me know that he felt his father was angry with him, but Alex couldn't pinpoint the reason. When I asked his parents about this they had no idea what he was talking about. Eventually we discovered that, the week before, Alex's parents had had an argument and Alex got caught in the middle. He had blamed himself for it ever since. Earth children tend to take on the role of peacemaker, and when they are unable to settle disputes, they blame themselves. In classical Chinese medicine, Earth is considered the middle, the intersection of the four directions and four seasons. This is why we find it right in the middle of the spectrum of five natures.

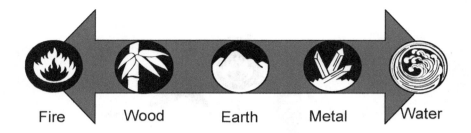

Fire   Wood   Earth   Metal   Water

We were eventually able to talk about his Earth powers, and his expression seemed to light up. Seeing how he fit in was critical to his being able to understand how to relate to the other kids in his class. This simple act seemed to provide him with great relief. Discovering that he didn't have to be like his Fire or Wood friends gave him some breathing room.

Bring Firelight into Your Earth Child's Life

Feeding the Earth puppy heart means creating the kind of joyful, light-hearted environment that will motivate your Earth child to focus in a more effective way. It's amazing how dramatically Earth children seem to respond to this. Getting caught up in the enthusiasm, they forget to think so much. I recommended that Alex's parents play a silly game before homework or on the way to school. This seemed to change his whole day.

Less Is Love

Alex's father was Fire natured. He was loud, fun, and unpredictable, and he recognized the power of his humor in lightening his son's mood. But he needed to learn that less is love. Sometimes being unpredictable is great for shaking your child out of his worries, but sometimes it can undermine his confidence. Making too sudden a shift from silliness to saying, "Okay now, let's get back to work" tended to add to Alex's worries, causing him to think that his father had shifted into anger at him. It's not uncommon for Earth children to become overly dependent on Fire's leadership without developing their own capacity to make decisions. Alex's father needed to learn how to step back too.

Previously, Alex had been doing his homework in his room alone. His concentration seemed to improve just by moving him into the kitchen, where he could feel like he was part of the family. (Incidentally, this didn't work at all for his brother, a Metal child who needed to go somewhere quiet to work.)

In the classroom, Alex's insecurity was highest when he was called on unexpectedly. Performance anxiety is a common complaint for many Earth children. Alex's father complained that while when they studied together, Alex seemed to know all the material, it seemed he went blank in the classroom. It took Alex several years to be comfortable speaking in public; but as with everything, when he had a little warm-up time he would do just fine.

Warming Up the Earth

Creating stronger feelings of security means meeting your child where he is. For Earth children, this means recognizing their need for sustained contact to feel secure. Before going to sleep, I had Alex's mother sit with him and massage his belly. The stomach is associated with Earth. His parents added some quiet music. Simply listening (and not thinking) is an important exercise for Earth children. Candlelight brings natural warmth and comfort during massages.

I recommended that his mother begin by rhythmically moving her hand in a clockwise fashion around his belly. It's best to keep to the rhythm of the music, allowing a child to focus on the movement of your hand and allow thoughts to come and go freely. This promotes secure sleep and relaxes tension in the diaphragm.

Centering the Stomach

Eating is a central feature to Earth's power. It is responsible for processing all the information (food) that we take in. Stagnation and accumulation of food is just like the obsessive thinking that goes nowhere in an insecure Earth child's mind. Alex's stomachaches were a big clue to his type of ADHD. I recommended that he avoid excessively cold foods (ice cream, raw foods) that slow digestion. Real comfort foods are traditionally soups and stews, not ice cream and cookies that children now crave when they're upset. There are a number of gentle Chinese herb formulas that I find helpful in "warming the middle" that help promote digestion and attention (see resources).

Training the Puppy Heart: The Power of Wood

Movement and direction characterize Wood's power. Alex's inactivity was a red flag for Earth stagnation. For Alex, daily movement became a very effective way of feeling a sense of progress. Physical movement improves body awareness and self-confidence and brings back a sense of being present in the world—the true strength of Earth. Many Earth children benefit from daily running. It's the perfect kind of low-pressure, meditative movement that gets a child out of her head and into her body. Other activities like yoga, bike riding, and swimming also improve focus.

I recommended that Alex spend more time in nature. Making a habit of hiking in the woods or working in a garden, even if it's for ten minutes a day, offers a natural context that reduces stress. Simply cutting down the amount of screen time, especially the passive entertainment of television, helped Alex tune in more actively to what was happening around him. Establishing this limit cut down on his mindless eating in front of the TV, a habit that tends to inhibit social connection.

Alex loved traveling with his family. Travel offers just the right mix of novelty (Fire) and movement (Wood) to stimulate the spirit of adventure. In fact, I find that many Earth children really mature when they're able to travel on their own. This forces them to stay focused, prioritize, and make decisions for themselves.

Earth Vision

Alex tended to get stuck in the middle of things. With too much to think about, too many decisions to make, and too many directions to choose from, his mind would get tied up in a knot. In Five Phase Correspondences, Wood commands our vision. It sets goals and shows us the path forward. Noticing Alex had difficulty crossing his eyes, I recommended he begin vision training therapy to strengthen his eye muscles. This greatly improved his reading speed and made homework less burdensome.

In fact, we discovered that, like many Earth children, Alex learned better when there were visual cues. Earth children often lose focus when they receive information out of context. Creating story maps that visually connect information helped him stay organized and improved retention (see diagram). Remember, it's connections that Earth children are most interested in. This helped him organize his thoughts when speaking, too.

Mapping a Storyline

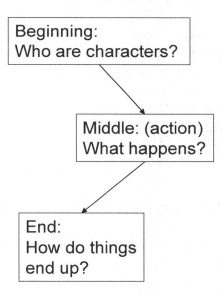

Setting concrete goals that are achievable is another kind of Wood activity that helped Alex raise his confidence and keep his eyes on the prize. Earth children who have become chronically insecure will forget where they are in their work and end up getting nowhere.

Less Is Love

The push of Wood reflects the kind of rugged individualism we hold in such high esteem in our country. This contrasts with Earth's preference to be a member of the group. Earth children are sometimes judged harshly for not being leaders. It's common for Wood-natured parents to lose patience with the indecisive Earth child. Remember, less is love. A little encouragement is good, but too much simply pushes the Earth child over the edge. Be aware of your expectations for your child. Learning to recognize the effects of your own sense of urgency is an important way to help the child you love succeed.

Even the expression the teacher used about Alex ("He's not living up to his potential") had a quality of judgment against him. Actually, it was his environment that wasn't living up to his potential! It turned out that Alex's stomachaches were directly related to the pressures of the standardized testing in school. He could feel the pressure his teacher was under and didn't want to let her down. But this just made it harder to think straight. Keeping quiet, he put all his stress in his stomach. Extra time on tests doesn't necessarily help in this situation. What needed to shift was the teacher's attitude about Alex. Training the puppy means creating opportunities for positive feedback to keep him engaged and moving forward.

Expanding the Big Heart: The Power of Metal

Earth gives birth to all the precious metals. Expanding the big heart means stimulating the full range of emotional experiences so that Alex would have an outlet for his sweet nature. Alex spent hours drawing. We used this to give him the chance to focus on details and patterns (Metal), such as different expressions of emotions. As a result, Alex began to organize stories in a more cohesive way. As his drawings got more elaborate, the positive feedback he got from friends and relatives helped his feeling of security.

Alex, like many Earth children who have lost confidence, didn't always believe the praise he was given. Luckily, Alex's father had a way of encouraging him to express himself through his art. He also created a routine (Metal) each night of sitting together to talk about the day. Rather than simply solving problems for his son, he got Alex to begin labeling his emotional states. This gradually helped break the vicious cycle of obsessive thinking. As Alex got better at describing his feelings more precisely, they were able to share their feelings and strengthen the bonds between them.

Earth Breathing

For Alex, learning to belly breathe had an immediate relaxing effect. The lungs are associated with Metal's powers of rhythm. Alex's parents learned to use this with him whenever they saw him becoming disorganized. In classical Chinese medicine, it is said that excessive thinking causes the qi (vital energy) to become tied up in a knot. Getting Alex to release his thoughts while breathing out and releasing his diaphragm helped redirect his focus when stressed and resolved his recurrent stomachaches.

Patterns and Rhythms

Using his skill at drawing, I introduced Alex to Pattern Games (see resources), which helped improve his ability to notice order and sequence. He began to show an interest in Legos, and I encouraged him to try copying complex designs. Alex loved bringing me completed projects each time he came for a visit. Toys like Legos are very popular these days, and they gave Alex the opportunity of getting positive feedback from his peers, which helped raise his confidence.

Alex later began using the Interactive Metronome, a perfect therapy for an Earth child to learn to balance movement (Wood) and rhythm (Metal). (See resources.) Later, this practice evolved into an interest in music. As he got older, his growing appreciation of different musical styles helped him widen his experience of subtle contrasts and similarities. A love of music also helped him maintain connections with other kids. Remember, music is a dominant mode of bonding and expression among teens.

A Diversity of Feelings

In order to expand the big heart, Alex needed to sort out his feelings. At the beginning, he didn't know *what* he was feeling. When asked what emotion was coming up, he'd simply say, "I don't know." His parents practiced labeling emotions with him every day. They would pause the DVD they were watching together or stop reading for a moment and ask him to identify the emotions of the characters. "What's that feeling, Alex: happy, sad, angry, afraid?" As he got better at identifying different emotions, Alex found that he wasn't being pulled in different directions when asked how he was feeling. He also found it easier to read others' emotional states more accurately. This helped him begin to see himself in a larger context.

I'm Hungry 1-2-3

Because digestion is central to Earth powers, Earth children often eat mindlessly. Alex began practicing identifying when he was hungry, part full, or totally full. His parents guided him to use the game I'm Hungry 1-2-3 to identify levels of feeling (see chapter 5). This brought greater attention to a range of inner states of being.

Mastering the Big Heart: The Power of Water

To become a true master of his Earth powers, Alex had to become more aware of how he was interacting with the world around him. I mapped the five relationships with him, which helped him appreciate his own power to channel Water (the deep mysteries of the world). We would return to this relationship again and again in our meetings together. Water represents the deep, concentrated meaning of things. Realizing that too much Earth can muddy Water's clarity was a difficult concept for him at first. As he became less self-involved, though, Alex began to see the effect he had on others. Muddy water means unclear thinking. Losing track of what he was saying, being too wishy-washy, annoyed others. Being worried about something that happened before or might happen later is not mastering the true power of being present. Learning how to avoid being swept away by thoughts can be a challenge for anyone, but it's a particular problem for the insecure Earth child. Meditation is a wonderful way to develop the power of presence.

Earth Meditation

This meditation can be done sitting or lying down.

1. To begin, have your child do a few belly breaths. Breathing in, the belly expands (not the chest); breathing out, the belly relaxes (letting go).

2. Now ask her to imagine that she is the ground that gives support to everything—the plants, the mountains, the rivers and seas. As she breathes into her belly, help her to imagine filling up with gravity. Ask her to think of herself as a balloon, big and round, but instead of being filled with air, have her imagine being filled with gravity or something heavy, like sand. Guide her to feel her weight increase.

3. On her next breath out, have her imagine that her breath is a stream running out to the sea. Ask her to try to steady the flow of the stream, letting go, releasing any tension in her body, feeling lighter.

4. As she breathes in, ask her to silently give thanks to the sky for giving her the air to breathe. Breathing out, she'll give thanks to the streams that move through her, keeping her from drying out.

I made a recording of this meditation for Alex, and he would play it on his iPod on the way to school. No one noticed him quietly holding his hand on his belly and breathing. He found doing a few belly breaths particularly helpful in clearing his mind before examinations. Focusing on exhalation strengthens the parasympathetic nervous system, reducing excessive sympathetic anxiety. Though his parents sometimes had to remind him to do his breathing exercises, they found that reducing Alex's anxiety improved his attention as well as his sleep and digestion.

To help with test-taking anxiety, I also recommended that Alex take a homeopathic remedy called *gelsemium* on test days. Homeopathy uses the power of dilution (Water) to neutralize specific symptoms and is very safe for children (see the resources for more on homeopathy). Taking this preparation on test days had the added benefit of giving Alex confidence and reminding him to stay centered before tests.

Feeling Earth's Gravity

Here is a guided meditation that may be particularly helpful for your Earth child the night before an exam:

1. Guide your child to do five belly breaths, releasing thoughts with each out-breath.

2. Ask her to notice her weight on the bed.

3. Have her begin by noticing the weight of her feet as she breathes in. Then she'll feel them become heavier as she breathes out. Let her know that this feeling means that she's connecting with Earth's gravity.

4. Guide her to slowly shift her attention to the weight of her legs, then her back, neck, shoulders, arms, and hands. She should take time to focus on meeting gravity at each part of the body.

Gravity prevents us from flying off into space. It holds us like a mother in her arms, creating a greater sense of safety. Gravity helps us feel the true power of presence in the world.

Earth Qigong Exercise: Standing Between Sky and Ground

This exercise is best done before homework, to help clear the mind of its clutter and improve organization.

1. Have your child stand with legs separated, shoulder-width apart, feet flat on the ground. She can imagine that she is the connection between the ground and sky.

2. As she faces straight forward, ask her to allow her gaze to focus on nothing in particular.

3. She'll start with her hands resting at her belly button. As she breathes into her belly (see basic belly-breathing exercise, chapter 5), ask her to raise one arm up above her head, as if she were holding up the sky. At the same time, her other arm pushes downward to her side, as if holding down the earth.

4. Have her hold her breath in this posture while stretching slightly, as if she were pushing both the sky and earth. She should keep her gaze focused forward and smile.

5. As she releases her breath, ask her to relax her body and allow her arms to return to the belly button. Repeat exercise, switching arms.

6. As you begin this practice, have her start with one or two breaths and work her way up over the weeks to twenty-five. As she practices, have her try to focus only on her posture and the movement of her breath.

Expanding Compassion

Developing mastery of Earth means being able to see the effect one has on others and experiencing a wide range of emotions, not just worry. Alex's greatest challenge was learning to work quietly by himself. He tended to be clingy and invade other people's space when he was insecure. He would fluctuate between being shy and talking excessively. Gradually he was able to learn how to read the signals that he was annoying others. Contemplative activities like chess helped promote his internal focus.

The Editing Game

Helping Alex to express his ideas in succinct terms defines the Earth-Water relationship. This meant getting to the point while keeping the listener interested. The Editing Game is very helpful in helping a child learn this balance.

We set the game up like this: Alex would get the most points for using the fewest words to tell the whole story. His parents practiced this with him until he got really good at being succinct.

You can also try reading poetry with your Earth child. Poetry helps improve creativity while condensing ideas into their most essential elements. I introduced Alex to haiku. We'd pick a subject, and he would have to come up with three lines (the rules, Metal) to express the whole meaning (Water). As he got better at this, his awareness seemed to be clearer.

Embracing Diversity: Becoming a True Caretaker of the World

Below are some activities parents, teachers, and therapists can work into homework assignments to help develop the Earth child's strengths:

- Find the hidden meaning in a piece of art, a piece of music, or a poem.

- Find a common theme in two stories (out of many, oneness).

- Find the meaning in a famous quote.

- Explain the meaning of "mystery" and "stillness."

- Describe one way of helping five different people.

- Read biographies of spiritual teachers (for instance, Gandhi, Muhammad, Jesus, Buddha).

- Explore cookbooks from other lands (helps develop diversity).

- Cook together to help strengthen your relationship.

- Create new recipes (promotes thinking outside the box).

Teaching the Earth Child

Finding a teacher who is lively (Fire) and encouraging (Wood) without being too stimulating or too pushy is not always possible. Metal-natured teachers who are very organized and predictable will help the Earth child stay on track. The biggest problem for the Earth child is having a teacher who doesn't even notice her. Even the slightest encouragement goes a long way for the Earth child. Make sure the teacher has a mechanism to offer positive feedback. Earth children build on small successes. Of course, the flip side is that they can spiral downward with a series of defeats. Creating a flowchart that emphasizes the progress your Earth child is making over the long run is the best way to keep her focused on the big picture. Teachers need to understand that Earth children learn by relationships. Presenting information in context will help your child get the most out of her lessons.

Alex Tuned In

By the time Alex got to high school, I would see him only when his worries got the best of him. With greater confidence, he was able to participate in activities that helped him be more outgoing. In fact, he discovered that the more he participated in class, the easier it was to pay attention. He recently began volunteering at the local animal shelter and says he wants to be a veterinarian when he grows up.

Here is another story about an Earth teenager who discovered her independence.

• *Gabriella: An Earth Teenager with ADHD*

Gabriella first came to see me with her mother when she was a junior in high school. Her mother was primarily concerned about Gabriella's physical appearance and complained that Gabriella was falling apart. She was short and slightly overweight in contrast to her mother, a tall, attractive woman who looked younger than her age. Gabriella told me that she thought she had ADD because all her friends were doing better than she was in school. She was terrified that she wasn't going to get into college. Her doctor had put her on a trial of stimulant medication, but it didn't do much. When she tried a higher dose, Gabriella just got more anxious. She had been healthy except for some allergies and occasional bloating. Her mother recently took her off wheat, but they were looking for more nutritional advice. After I described the five natures, Gabriella and her mother agreed that Gabriella had "a lot of Earth and a little Metal" in her. She loved routines but sometimes got a little stuck in them.

The pressure on juniors in high school these days is enormous. I see many children burn out just when they're supposed to shine the brightest. Gabriella complained that she was unable to sleep because she simply had too many thoughts in her head. She just wanted something to make it easier to get through all her work.

Gabriella and her mom both seemed very impatient to fix the problem. Gabriella identified her mother as being Fire natured. She had been a model before having kids and had recently thrown herself into the study of nutrition. Interestingly, Gabriella's main obsession seemed to be food. She talked a lot about "good" and "bad" foods and privately told me that she would eat bad food when she was nervous. She was frightened that her mother would find out and be upset.

We began by discussing ways to pay attention to hunger and fullness. I explained that we could use this awareness to help her improve her attention. I suggested that she increase the diversity in her diet. Specifically, we talked about adding more protein and eating less dairy. I feared that her high dairy intake may have been adding to her feeling of dissatisfaction. After all, I told her, she wasn't a baby calf. She agreed to give it a try. We arranged a series of acupuncture sessions during which we would practice meditations to help her focus on her body and let go of her thoughts. On certain acupuncture points I placed special magnets that she wore during the day at school. These points were chosen to help regulate her anxiety. She began taking some gentle Chinese herbs to help regulate her digestion as well.

We talked about her special nature and the fact that she didn't have to be like everyone else. I encouraged Gabriella to join the local gym her mother belonged to, but she told me she felt like she was competing with her mother. Gabriella began going to a yoga studio, and I advised her mother not to join her there (much to her dismay). Our regular visits together allowed us to work on strategies to improve her organizational skills. We also talked about the Five Phase Correspondences, and realizing that her nature was different from that of her friends had a liberating effect on her. I encouraged her to plan a summer activity away from home. This was a big deal for her, as she'd never been able to go away. She chose to take a summer course at a college in another state.

At the last minute she came to see me because she didn't think she could do it. We reviewed all her breathing techniques and I made a CD for her of the "Feeling Gravity" guided meditation that she put on her iPod and listened to each night. Her mother was very doubtful that Gabi would go, and I talked separately with her about the ways her body language was undermining Gabi's confidence.

Gabriella did manage to make it to the out-of-state college, but she had a rocky start. I got one call at the beginning of summer from her mother telling me that Gabriella had been crying every night and she was considering bringing her home. I urged her to wait another few days and Gabi and I had a long conversation on the phone. We reviewed all her exercises again, and Gabriella seemed to calm down. It was clear that she wanted to succeed in this. That was the last I heard from them all summer. Her mother called me once the following school year to let me know that Gabriella had gotten into the college. She was eager to go and her mother thanked me for my help. She said she felt that she'd learned as much about herself as she had about Gabi through the entire process.

Loving Our Earth Children

Earth children sit at the center of our lives. Their teaching is sweetness and caring. We might feel sorry for the Earth child because she gets so easily pushed around. But when she feels secure, when her big heart is strong, she can be depended on in any situation. The Earth child channels all the deep wisdom of Water into our world. She offers an outlet for the excitement of Fire. She becomes the challenge for Wood to motivate. And she gives birth to all the patterns of Metal, giving context to all the myriad ways we humans can express ourselves. In so doing, this child, with her Earth superpower of relationships, helps us ripen our own nature. For it is through our connections that we find a home, that central place that she has attentively prepared for us to live in.

A Summary of the Approach to Earth

- **Feeding the Puppy Heart:** Lighten up with Fire. Use humor and play, sensory integration, and belly massage.

- **Training the Puppy Heart:** Use Wood by coaching, setting goals, mapping out stories and activities, and increasing movement. Increase protein in the diet and try vision therapy.

- **Expanding the Big Heart:** Metal provides an outlet. Use arts and crafts, music, The Pattern Game, breathing exercises, and reading others' emotions.

- **Mastering the Big Heart:** Cultivate Water for clarity and depth. Practice qigong exercise, self-reflection meditation, and activities that help embrace diversity.

Chapter 9

The Metal Child

Maria

Maria is a lean young girl with sharp features, high cheekbones, a long nose, and an intense gaze. I have had the privilege of knowing her since she was a baby in my pediatric practice. She has always had a particular way of doing things. Even as a very young child she had an uncanny ability to see patterns everywhere and loved doing puzzles and drawing intricate designs. Her mother, a bright, cheerful woman who had been born in South America, always knew her daughter was special. But when Maria was approaching fourth grade, her mother began to panic that there might be something wrong with her. Maria had suffered from bouts of asthma, which had decreased in recent years. When Maria began preschool, her mother noticed how different Maria's behavior was from the other children's. Maria had become fixated on trains and tended to exclude the other children. She'd often come home in a bad mood, set off by some little thing another child had said. I had very little contact with Maria's father. Her mother and I met several times to discuss ways to encourage social interactions and, over time, Maria made good progress.

In fourth grade, when the work began getting harder, Maria began getting stuck. The teacher was concerned that she might have a neurologic problem. Maria seemed out of sync with the rest of the class. She would ask a question about something that had happened hours before. She was also having problems socializing again. She tattled on other children for doing things they weren't supposed to do. On more than one occasion the teacher had to tell Maria that she wasn't in charge of the class. Maria would get very insulted and then refuse to participate in anything. She had become increasingly sensitive to criticism, claiming the teacher was wrong. She'd complain that she didn't like any of the other kids and would go on and on about what was bad about each of them. She found it increasingly hard to let things go, constantly blaming someone when things went wrong. Her nighttime routines had become elaborate rituals that were interfering with her ability to fall asleep. Maria's mother was also worried that her asthma had started acting up again, and she wasn't sure whether this was triggering these behaviors or whether the stress of school was triggering the asthma.

Mapping a Solution

When we met and mapped out Maria's characteristics, her mother (a Fire-natured woman) knew right away that Maria was a Metal child. This was a great revelation for her. Just being able to talk about Maria's nature in a more positive, nonjudgmental way reassured her.

Maria's attention problems came from getting stuck when things didn't go according to plan—*her* plan. She found it hard to see the forest for the trees. This rigidity only exaggerated her puppy-heart expressions, making it impossible for her to see the big picture. Her powers of precision amplified into narrow, rigid attention.

In mapping out solutions for Maria's problems with attention, we looked at the four principal strategies for helping the Metal child:

Mapping a Solution for Metal

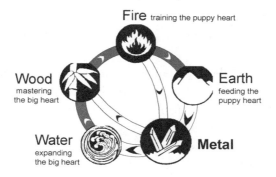

Feeding the Puppy Heart: The Power of Earth

The first step was getting Maria's mother to recognize that ADHD symptoms are a cry for help. In order to be able to create a deeper sense of security for Maria, we had to acknowledge who Maria was and how she processed the world. Earth nourishes Metal, and Earth represents the power of context and relationships. Maria wanted to fit in, but she wasn't sure how to. I encouraged Maria and her mother to begin slowly with one-on-one playdates with a class-mate. Having even one friend in the classroom can become an anchor of security in what feels like chaos to a Metal child.

Maria had a friend who happened to be taking an aikido class, and I suggested that Maria join. The sensei (teacher) was someone I knew to be friendly and fair and he encouraged group cohesiveness (Earth nature). Though Maria was rather physically awkward, she loved the structure of the class and her sensei discovered creative ways to help Maria feel like she was an important member of the group. This became her first real taste of belonging.

Because eating is a big part of Earth activities, Maria and her mother began cooking together. Her mother was able to show Maria how to use her "special powers" to follow recipes exactly while gradually exploring different spices and flavors. Maria had always had a keen sense of smell, becoming hypersensitive when she was stressed. Certain scents would trigger her wheezing, too. Her mother told me that she was able to gauge Maria's sense of security at any given time by the way she approached cooking. If Maria had had a bad day, she would get stuck in some simple task like peeling potatoes. Maria's mother would gently point out Maria's behavior in these moments, and they became an opportunity for Maria to connect her feelings to reactions that were tangible.

I also emphasized the importance of eating together. For years Maria had eaten separately from her parents, and this lack of connection around food had increased her rigidity. She had always been very sensitive to the way food was presented. If a meal didn't look right, she wouldn't touch it. Initially, eating together was a very stressful experience for everyone. Maria tried to control how the food looked on everyone's plate. But that spring her mother made a great discovery: Maria could taste the difference between local organic food and the processed foods sold at the supermarket. She used this as an opportunity to join a local food co-op, and she and Maria began helping sort the vegetables and fruits that came from the farms. Maria really enjoyed this and even wrote a rather righteous sixth-grade report on the virtues of supporting local farming. Interestingly, Maria's mother felt that eating organic food seemed to reduce her allergies and asthma attacks as well.

Preparing food with her mother also helped reduce Maria's aversions to certain smells and textures. As she experienced context and relationship in cooking and eating, Maria's hypersensitivity decreased. Eating together became a place to discuss the merits of the food in a more positive way. Making this a daily routine helped reinforce her sense of safe haven, reducing the intensity of her puppy-heart rigidity.

Making Earth Contact

Working in a garden promotes a direct connection with Earth power. The gradual growth process makes imperfections less threatening. After all, a tomato that's not perfectly round may still taste really great. Maria seemed to have a green thumb. She eventually took over her mother's flower garden and then turned it into a vegetable garden (much more functional to her). She would bring me the most amazing vegetables whenever she'd come for visits in the fall.

Maintaining contact for Maria doesn't mean the same thing that it does to other children. Maria's mom was particularly good at creating space for her daughter to feel connected without feeling invaded. She didn't demand that Maria maintain eye contact, even though that was one of the complaints from Maria's school. Maria's mom recognized that pressure to keep eye contact only increased Maria's sense of insecurity. Maria would get most overwhelmed when she felt her boundaries threatened, and her mother was careful to make subtle shifts in her own body language in order to maintain a sense of security in contact. Just keeping a hand on Maria's shoulder when she was getting stuck helped Maria loosen up a little.

Maria was initially wary of getting acupuncture. I let her use a needle on me first (a technique I use with most children), and she eventually felt secure enough to try it for herself. The first few sessions involved using only a single needle, to help her develop a sense of trust. Gradually, she became more curious about these sessions with me. It helped her connect to feelings in her body, and we would use this to help shift her attention. Eventually she would be able to tell her mom exactly when she thought she needed a treatment—a good sign of increasing self-awareness. Incidentally, Maria also got very good at telling me *exactly* where the needles should go.

Being an Earth Parent for Your Metal Child

Creating a secure base for a Metal child like Maria takes great patience for any parent. Rigidity can make the simplest task a battle. Maria had the habit of pointing out her parents' inconsistencies. Her mother had to learn to see this as a cry for help and not to take it personally. Maria's father, a kind though passive Earth-natured man, recognized this behavior as a reflection of Maria's nature and saw that she was just as hard on herself when she made mistakes. Both of Maria's parents began to take these behaviors as signals that Maria needed a little more support. They would shift their body language to get closer (but not too close) and remind her that they loved her regardless of the mistakes she made. They let her know that they appreciated her keen perception, honoring her nature. This simple message of unconditional love has a special power to create the kind of security that allows a child to gradually let go of rigid preconceptions. But remember: don't overwhelm your Metal child with too much touchy-feely talk. Simple, direct, and clear acknowledgments work best.

Training the Puppy Heart: The Power of Fire

Simply indulging Maria's nature was not enough. Training the puppy heart means offering a secure path forward. Fire melts Metal's rigidity, making intimacy and engagement with the world possible. Maria's mother had a natural way of lightening up Maria's mood with humor, though Maria's father didn't always get this. He tended to take offense at her refusal to do things his way and this only further confused Maria. He needed to learn how to get Maria to laugh at herself without being insulted. This isn't always easy to do with Metal children. It takes time and starts by being able to acknowledge the characteristics of one's nature. Maria actually had a wonderful, dry sense of humor. Her parents learned how to develop this humor by using things she found funny when she was stressed.

The Art of Expression

Making verbal contact was tricky for Maria. When she was insecure, she'd often misinterpret cues. Training the puppy heart means offering positive feedback to improve intimacy and foster connection. Maria's father had to learn that less is love. He tended to talk too much, and this felt like an intrusion to Maria. He made more of an effort to spend quiet time with her, offering consistent, positive, nonverbal cues (a smile, a wink) when she was able to shift from rigidity to connection. He realized he had been overwhelming her with both excessive praise and criticism.

The Reading Emotions Game

Maria tended to take things too literally. She'd get stuck on certain words and miss the intention, causing further insecurity. I recommended that her parents take pictures of each other making as many expressions as they could think of. They put these in a book and regularly practiced with Maria in labeling them. Gradually, she got better at identifying different emotional expressions and this helped her learn the rules of nonverbal communication. But as we will see later, learning the rules of reading emotions was only the first step in training Maria's attention. It takes time to discover that the map is not the territory.

Singing Together

Maria's parents discovered that she had perfect pitch when she sang along with recordings, but she struggled when it came to singing with real people. She tended to dominate, singing louder than everyone else in an effort to tune out what she perceived as their mistakes. They began practicing singing together every night as a family. Developing an ear for harmonizing helped Maria learn that she wasn't always the center of attention. The give-and-take of songs gradually became more fun (Fire) as she learned to loosen her hold and trust the connections with others (Earth).

Fire Massage

Maria's mother began doing deep massage each night on her child. Metal children are prone to muscle tightness and dry skin. Massaging with warm, scented flower oils helped Maria relax at the end of a day. Her mom discovered hard knots at the back of Maria's neck and shoulder blades and was careful not to overdo the massage. If she did, Maria would complain that it felt like she was being invaded, a feeling that undermined her sense of security. Another way we used Maria's acute sense of smell was to apply a drop of cedarwood essential oil behind her ear during the day. This helped her remain present and relaxed. (See appendix for more suggestions for essential oils.) But remember, less is love. It's very easy to overwhelm a Metal child with too many odors. It's not uncommon for perfumes to become so distracting that a child can no longer focus.

Sensory Integration

Training the puppy heart means creating a secure path out of the emergency state. I often recommend sensory therapy, which can help a child engage in the changing external world without getting stuck. Remember, change is the very thing that often triggers puppy-heart insecurities in Metal children. Fire represents the sensory experience of change. Maria began wearing a weighted jacket to help her feel grounded (Earth) and secure in the midst of change (Fire) (see resources).

As Maria became more comfortable with our sessions, we began using emWave feedback to bring heart (Fire) and respiration (Metal) into coherence. This treatment began to balance those internal rhythms so critical to stability for Metal (see resources).

I Spy Something New

Maria's parents recognized that her attention problems were linked to her natural tendency to get overwhelmed with change. Rather than blaming her, they began to make her feel more comfortable with change by playing a game in which they'd take turns scanning a room looking for something that had changed. We call this I Spy Something New. Because Maria had such a good eye for noticing detail, she readily participated. Gradually, she got used to seeing change as fun rather than a threat.

The Silly Mistake Game

It was Maria's nature to take things very seriously. While there's nothing inherently wrong with that, it can sometimes set up a vicious cycle. When Maria made mistakes it magnified her feelings of chaos and insecurity, which then made her overly sensitive to the tiniest mistakes. To break this cycle, I played The Silly Mistake Game with her. We each took turns drawing a picture, consciously making an effort to make a single mistake. She was great at finding my mistakes but had a hard time creating a mistake herself. However, she was gradually able to loosen up enough to get very good at hiding mistakes and seeing whether I could find them. This lightened the whole idea of right and wrong while honoring her innate abilities.

Silly Metaphors: How Is a This Like a That?

Metaphor and analogy require a leap beyond rigid labels. This was extremely challenging for Maria. Fire melts Metal's boundaries. Catching moments when Maria was not so rigid, her mother would play a game with her that I call How Is a This Like a That? Taking turns, they would randomly pick two objects in a room and look for ways that they were alike. For example, if you choose a tree and a person, you can point out that both have arms, that roots are like legs, and so on. Maria's mom tried to keep the game lighthearted and a little absurd. She watched for signs that Maria was getting stuck and would back off if she saw Maria struggling. Gradually, Maria got better at identifying more abstract relationships (like the feelings of others), a sign that she was expanding her big heart.

Expanding the Big Heart: The Power of Water

When Maria was most stuck, she needed a way out, a release from her own Metal cage. Being stuck is a terrible feeling. I call it "constipation of the mind." The compulsive puppy heart limits attention to a very rigid perspective. Expanding the big heart means opening up to a broader range of emotional experiences. This can free up attention to be more flexible and improves adaptibility to the changing flow of circumstances. Metal gives birth to Water, and Water represents the flow of nature. Beneath its surface, water holds the deep mysteries of time and space that run through life.

The Subtle Ecology of Space: Feng Shui

We used Maria's sensitivity to subtle changes in her environment as medicine. *Feng shui* is the ancient Chinese practice of using the environment to influence one's health and well-being. Maria said that when they painted one wall in her bedroom red, it helped her get up on the right side of the bed for school. We made a game out of routinely changing the position of the things in her room. She could choose where items and furniture would go, with the understanding that it was only a temporary change. Realizing that there can be routine within change allowed Maria to begin to develop a greater sense of security in diversity. In fact, Maria embraced the power of change by using her keen eye to study the science of feng shui and later pointed out how things should be placed in my office, too.

The Mystery of Time

In reviewing Maria's early childhood history with her parents, we realized that her grandfather's death when she was four years old had had a profound effect on Maria. Her grandfather had died unexpectedly. At the time, Maria had struggled to understand why people die, and she became quietly fixated on death for many years. She was able to describe death to me as a kind of injustice. I suggested that her parents consider getting her involved in the church her mother belonged to. Parents often think it strange when, as a doctor, I write a prescription recommending religion for their child. But that's just what I did for Maria, and she took her burgeoning spirituality very seriously. Her mother was a deeply spiritual person and was delighted to introduce her to that world. In church, Maria was able to find a belief system and a code of ethics that satisfied her need to know why. In fact, Maria's mother enthusiastically began introducing her to other religions as well, and this understanding eventually helped her embrace a greater tolerance for diversity.

The Power of Traditions

I also encouraged Maria to take a more active role in her family's holiday traditions, particularly those that marked the passage of time. Losing these traditions can cut us off from the wisdom passed down through the generations. Holidays like Solstice, Christmas, and Passover offer a way out of stress by giving a sense of constancy in the midst of the great mystery of change.

Maria developed a strong relationship with her grandmother even though she lived in another country. Whenever they visited her family in South America, Maria had a chance to stay with her grandmother for extended periods of time. Fostering such an important connection seemed to have a profound effect on Maria's abilities to interact in school each time she returned. She would find comfort in looking at old pictures of the family with her parents, and this helped her feel less isolated and gain a greater perspective on her heritage. Through this connection Maria gained a greater sense of her own identity. Her mother developed this into a practice of reviewing joyful events whenever Maria was feeling stressed. Simply recounting stories is one of the ways the big heart empowers us to see things in a larger context. It also helped Maria practice how to structure a good story without getting stuck in the details.

Realizing that memory is a deeply personal thing gave Maria the chance to recognize that we don't all remember the same event in exactly the same way. This realization helped Maria embrace diversity, generating a greater understanding of others' experiences and reducing her black-and-white view of the world.

Maria became an avid reader at an early age. When she discovered the *Harry Potter* books, she had endless dialogue with me in the office about the subtle details of the characters. In fact, she was able to identify each of the characters according to their Five Phase natures. Her interest in the popular series also helped her connect to peers.

Water Support

Winter was challenging for Maria. She was sensitive to the excessive dry heat in her house and the long hours indoors made her excessively reactive, both psychologically and physically. I suggested Maria make a routine of taking baths with a drop of lavender oil to help her unwind at the end of the day or even before studying. I also encouraged her to drink a lot of water in the winter, as proper water intake is essential for the healthy function of lungs and skin.

The Natural Wonder of Shades

The more time Maria spent outside, the more relaxed she became. She loved going to the beach and was much less rigid on vacations there. She became an avid collector of stones and shells, which helped shift her focus toward a greater tolerance of the diversity found in nature rather than rigid perfection. Through her love of patterns she improved her ability to describe the subtle difference in shapes and colors that lay beyond rigid ideas of good and bad, black and white.

Trusting Intuition

One of Maria's biggest challenges was learning how to know things intuitively, not just analytically. This took careful training. Studies have shown that intuition helps us solve problems with greater creativity (Jung-Beeman et al. 2004). Maria's mother, being very intuitive, didn't understand how her daughter couldn't trust her own feelings. When her father brought home a dog from the pound, Maria was encouraged to take part in the training. This helped expand her perspective on reading impulses. Dogs have a natural playfulness that encourages us to imagine what they're feeling. When Maria's father asked, "What do you think he wants?" and Maria responded, they were exploring feelings as they were happening rather than just in pictures. Maria's parents came to realize that using imagination and trusting impressions took practice for Maria.

Maria's mother began playing a game with her of reading together in front of a mirror, allowing expressions to evolve naturally. When her mother caught Maria smiling she would use this opportunity to help Maria identify her emotions, asking, "Are you happy right now?" Gradually, Maria began to make deeper connections between outer appearances and inner feelings. Guessing what her mother was feeling helped her associate her own expressions with her mother's, and the positive feedback she got from correctly sensing her mother's emotions encouraged her to keep practicing.

Chanting

Realizing that Maria needed a way to explore her own intuition, I suggested that she and her mother chant "Ommm" together. Chanting can open up a space where the inner narrator recedes, allowing "messages" to emerge on their own. The practice creates room for the emergence of feelings and nonanalytical thoughts. Chanting whenever they had the chance, Maria was able to directly experience intuition. She would describe these experiences with the same kind of precision and enthusiasm she had when she found a new shell on the beach.

Dreaming

Discussing her dreams was another opportunity to expand Maria's big heart. Maria began keeping a journal of her dreams, and each Sunday she would sit with her mother to discuss their possible meanings. At first this was extremely challenging for Maria, but over time her exploration of the metaphorical language of her inner landscape improved.

Exploring the World

Maria's parents found that traveling expanded her flexibility and improved her attention. When she was very young, Maria hadn't liked going to new places. However, her parents made Maria a part of the planning as she got older, giving her a greater sense of control. The novelty of new experiences encouraged her to break out of old routines. Avoiding rigid itineraries, she began to discover that the map was not the territory.

Mastering The Big Heart: The Power of Wood

Mastery of Metal manifests in its relationship with Wood. Maria ultimately needed to become more aware of the effect she was having on those around her. This is a key to developing deeper self-reflection in the Metal child.

Wood relates to how we move through challenges to achieve goals. Maria had a tendency to be overly critical of the way others did things, and learning to go with the flow was very challenging.

Mastery over Movement

Maria became more serious about her aikido class and found it a welcome relief from excessive mental activity. Her dad joined the class with her and found that this group activity (Earth) helped strengthen their relationship. Maria particularly enjoyed the structure of the class and was very proud of her progress. With time, Maria found it easier to regulate her attention in group settings. With physical contact, she became more aware of when she was stiffening up and how it made others feel uncomfortable. Activities like dance and yoga helped her learn how to counterbalance this stiffness with subtle changes in her position, relaxing her body. This ability to loosen her posture and ease her movements made it easier for her to relate to other children.

Breathing exercises are particularly important in loosening up Metal's rigid control, thereby regulating stress. The lungs are associated with Metal and muscles are associated with Wood. Learning to coordinate these helps unlock the diaphragm and promote relaxation. Making breathing exercises an integral part of introspective meditation helped keep Maria in touch with the basic rhythms of life.

Metal Meditation

This meditation can be done sitting or lying down.

1. To begin, have your child do a few belly breaths. As he breathes in, his belly expands (not the chest). As he breathes out, his belly relaxes (letting go).

2. Now ask your child to imagine that he is a green mountain. He is solid and strong on the ground, pointing straight up to the sky. As he breathes in, guide him to feel the earth's gravity move right down into his belly. He should feel himself get heavy and solid while breathing in.

3. As he breathes out, ask him to let go of the sky and feed the wild trees growing on his mountainside. Remind him to feel himself become lighter as he breathes out.

4. As he breathes in, ask him to silently give thanks to the earth for making him so solid. Breathing out, have him give thanks to the trees that keep him sheltered in green all year long.

Metal Qigong Exercise: Standing Like a Mountain

This exercise is best done in the evening (facing west) before dinner, but it can be practiced anytime to help loosen focus and refresh the mind.

1. Ask your child to stand with legs separated as widely as is comfortable, feet flat on the ground. His hands will be on his hips. Now have him imagine that he is a tall mountain reaching up into the clouds.

2. Ask him to face straight forward and to look at nothing in particular.

3. Have him take a breath into his belly (see chapter 5). Ask him to bend forward at the waist as he breathes out so that he's facing the ground.

4. Breathing in again, he will slowly raise his body up and then twist slightly to the right. Ask him to hold his breath and feel the flexibility of his body. Have him try to smile.

5. As he releases his breath, guide him to relax his body. While his hands are still on his hips, have him swivel gently back and bend forward to the ground. Repeat breathing in and turning to the left side.

6. Start your child off with one or two breaths and then he can work his way up over the weeks to twenty-five. As he practices, ask him to try to focus only on his posture and the movement of his breath.

Expanding Compassion

Ultimately, Maria needed to move beyond mere maps and rules of social engagement to actually experiencing emotional exchanges. Being able to see through another's eyes is a powerful way of mastering the big heart. Acting out roles allowed Maria to experience other perspectives. Her wonderful memory and attention to detail made her a great acting student. She began taking part in the drama club at school, and her mother took this opportunity to help her "feel" different characters.

Maria gained greater perspective by comparing how she felt one day to how she felt the next. Through this practice she learned to question why she reacted in certain ways in certain circumstances. Being able to identify when she got stuck gave her a chance to anticipate this possibility and catch the feelings as they emerged. Working in the controlled setting of a social-skills group, she was able to try out different, more creative emotional responses that allowed her to better negotiate conflict.

Embracing Diversity: Becoming a True Judge in the World

Below are some activities parents, teachers, and therapists can work into homework assignments to help develop the Metal child's strengths:

- Explain the meaning of "change" and "adventure."

- Describe three situations in which change was good.

- Come up with a story that has as many endings as you can.

- Create a map for an activity and then put it into action. Compare your feelings making the map and experiencing the adventure.

- Social action: Come up with three ways you would change the world for the better.

- Come up with a way to make fair decisions in the classroom.

- Construct a decision tree for an activity, mapping choices and consequences. Try three different examples.

- The next time the family takes a vacation, leave your lodgings every day for something unexpected. That is, no plans—just leave the room and see what happens out in the world.

- Read biographies of famous explorers, inventors, and entrepreneurs.

Teaching the Metal Child

Finding the right teacher for Maria was always a challenge. With so many rules and requirements, school has its own "Metal" rigidity. This can lead to clashes of routines. Learning to contend with diverse teaching styles, not to mention the academic and social pressures that are on the rise these days, is a tremendous source of stress for the Metal child. Finding a teacher who can use your child's love of patterns and aesthetic sense is invaluable. It's often best to meet with teachers at the beginning of the year to clue them in to your child's particular style of learning. When a Metal child's interests are validated, a teacher can coax him to relax and embrace the joy of learning much more effectively.

As Metal children tend to get so caught up in details, it will be helpful for teachers to encourage a more Earth-based focus on relationships and context. Learning through comparisons and analogy is a great way of promoting deeper understanding of abstract concepts in the Metal child. This leads to greater potential for problem solving. Even learning a second language seems to help Metal children embrace diversity ("You mean there's more than one way to say something?"). Many Metal children have a natural affinity for science and math, and teachers can reinforce these interests, thus improving self-esteem.

Just as parents need to work with their own particular predispositions, it's important for teachers to be aware of their own rigid habits. Teachers are under enormous pressure these days to meet specific demands and standards of education. This can severely limit their creativity and add too much Metal to a Metal child's life. Locking horns with a rigid child about some trivial way of doing something never succeeds. Learning to let go first and lighten up the mood models the kind of behavior that will encourage a Metal child's flexibility. Wood-natured teachers must be aware that pushing a stressed Metal child who is set in his ways will have little or no effect, and punishing him will only harden his resolve. A teacher who can offer clear instructions with plenty of advance preparation and consistent positive feedback will command more respect.

It's important that the teacher of a Metal child pay attention to the child's development of social relationships. Peers are an important source of security and help shape tolerance and empathy. Encouraging solid friendships in the early years of a Metal child's life will have perhaps a more profound effect on learning than teaching reading or writing. Daily challenges often arise outside the field of the teacher's attention. A monitor may need to pay special attention to "free time" activities on the playground or on the bus, where there are no fixed rules. These are often the places of greatest stress for the Metal child.

Maria Tuned In

Maria has made amazing progress in just a few years. As her confidence has improved, her attention has become less rigid and she's become more successful, both academically and socially. She has recently set up a science-fiction club at school and delights in organizing events with other members. She continues to move up in ranking in her martial arts practice and has recently become involved in competitive swimming, winning awards for her diving skills. She has managed to make a few solid friendships that have helped her learn the value of compromise and trust. She continues to take her visits for acupuncture very seriously and she has been studying Chinese, often correcting my pronunciation of the acupuncture points.

Here's a story about a Metal teenager who learned how to develop his powers into real magic.

• *Brett: A Metal Teenager with ADHD*

Brett first came to me when he was fourteen years old. He was suffering from terrible tics and was failing a number of subjects in his first year of high school. The tics began to get worse at the onset of puberty. He had seen several specialists and was taking an antidepressant for obsessive-compulsive symptoms. His parents wanted a second opinion on natural ways to treat his tics and attention issues. After my first session with Brett, he was delighted to figure out that he was Metal natured. It was the first time anyone had acknowledged his style as something other than a problem. He particularly liked my appreciation of his sense of humor. He had managed to memorize the complete *Monty Python* skits and would drop into one of these whenever there was a lull in conversation.

I started by teaching him a series of breathing exercises, focusing on rhythm and physical presence. I directed acupuncture at balancing his Metal-Wood conflicts. He seemed to enjoy the powerful sensations acupuncture produced, and we used this awareness to focus his mind on shifting feelings. I also introduced him to magic tricks, which he took to with a passion. He became so proficient at these that it helped his popularity in school. As he got older, he even volunteered to entertain disabled children. Much to everyone's delight, he became quite the showman and what's more, all his tics seemed to vanish during his performance.

Brett had suffered from chronic constipation ever since he was young. It's not uncommon for Metal children to get "stuck" around the time of toilet training. Getting him to drink warm tea rather than ice-cold soda and to avoid overly processed foods helped keep things flowing. Adding flaxseed oil and evening primrose oil (rich in omega-3 fatty acids) helped his bowel, lung, and brain function. Homeopathy was also very helpful in controlling his tics and loosening up his tendency to hyperfocus (see appendix). Developing a regular rhythm of bowel function had a powerful effect on Brett's mood and attention. He literally had a load off his mind.

Brett also suffered from terrible sleep problems. If his routine was off or things hadn't gone according to plan during the day, he found it impossible to fall asleep. He began taking a low dose of melatonin (1 mg) to help him ease into sleep. The cycle of dreams is particularly helpful in supporting parasympathetic "rest and digest" functions. Getting enough sleep and dream time allowed him to wake more refreshed and break the vicious cycle of fatigue. Dreaming is an important way we integrate our diverse experiences using the language of metaphor. Brett found that if he had a regular bowel movement and got a good night's sleep, his tics were virtually nonexistent and it was much easier to pay attention in school. It may be hard to believe, but such simple solutions allowed him to eventually be weaned off his medications.

Brett went on to truly challenge himself. His growing interest in having friends led him to join a teen group traveling in the western states. This strengthened his self-confidence, making him more aware of his own abilities to meet unexpected challenges. Brett is now in college, where he's studying philosophy, and he hopes to one day become a lawyer.

Embracing the Virtues of Metal

Metal plays a vital role in our lives. Its virtues bring order to the chaos of change (Fire) and allow us to work as a group (Earth). Metal becomes the matrix through which we can make sense of the mysteries of the world (Water), and it ultimately offers a map that allows us to reach our goals (Wood). Many of the greatest minds of science embraced Metal virtues. People like Charles Darwin and Louis Pasteur, who meticulously studied the order and pattern of life, have expanded our understanding of the world we live in and have given us greater control over our own destiny.

A Summary of the Approach to Metal

- **Feeding the Puppy Heart:** Use Earth strategies to promote contact. These include massage, working with analogy, reading emotions, cooking, gardening, and singing.

- **Training the Puppy Heart:** Fire-focused strategies include encouraging humor, play-acting, sensory integration, trusting intuition, I Spy Something New, silly metaphors, and The Silly Mistake Game.

- **Expanding the Big Heart:** Water strategies help us to explore the unknown. Try delving into mystery, religion, magic, collecting, keeping a dream journal, and swimming.

- **Mastering the Big Heart:** Use Wood to encourage movement. Use breathing exercises, self-reflection on how one's body language affects others, travel, and activities to help become a true alchemist of the world.

Chapter 10

The Water Child

Jack

When I first met Jack, a small, thick-boned nine-year-old boy with a broad forehead and dark circles under his eyes, he had an air of diffidence and appeared to have no idea why he'd been brought in to see me. His mother, who was annoyed by his lack of awareness, had come to me because Jack was refusing to go to school. His teachers had complained that he hadn't turned in any assignments in months. She told me that he had lost all interest in the work. His teacher had referred him to the school counselor because she thought he seemed depressed.

Jack's mother described him as having been born "an old man." She told me he'd always been a bit of a curmudgeon and a loner in the family. As a young child, he would spend hours playing with toy dinosaurs in his room. His hearing and speech had been evaluated when he was three years old because he seemed to be lost in his own world. By the time he was six, his speech had eventually caught up. He was taken to a neurologist because of concerns that his staring spells might be seizures, but the results of an EEG (brain scan) were normal. Jack had been to the pediatrician several times because of a lack of energy, but the workups revealed nothing. Jack's parents started him on several vitamins they'd found at the health food store, but that didn't seem to make a difference. When they told the doctor that he was struggling to keep up in school, the physician suggested that Jack might have some kind of ADD.

Time had always been Jack's greatest challenge. He had always moved slowly. His mother told me that whenever he felt pushed, he slowed down even more. She was concerned that he was becoming more withdrawn, spending hours in his room reading books about black magic and witchcraft.

In meeting with Jack's mother and father, I discussed Jack's deep, intro-spective nature, which they both agreed sounded like the Water child. Water-natured children dance to the beat of a different drummer, one that the classroom doesn't seem able to accommodate. We agreed that, if his problems weren't addressed, Jack would be at real risk for alienation and depression. At the following meeting, Jack sat and pondered the spectrum of five natures for a long time in what appeared to be absent-minded silence. Then, just as I was about to interrupt his reverie and ask him again which powers he thought he had, he blurted out, "I'm a Water child." And so we mapped out a solution like this:

Mapping a Solution for Water

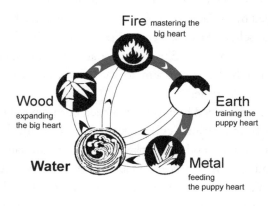

Feeding the Puppy Heart: The Power of Metal

Feeling rushed in a world that gave him no time for the kind of deep contemplation his nature desired, Jack was bound to feel insecure. But this insecurity was expressed in a particular way. Jack withdrew and became apathetic. Finding ways to make a Water child feel more secure about herself once she's "left the planet" can be a daunting task for parents. Metal feeds Water, just as a mountain gives birth to a stream. The first step was to ensure that Jack's environment was consistent. This is the true power of Metal, and it meant that Jack's parents needed to change their own habits. Ever since he was an infant, there had been no routines at home. Jack's siblings created a kind of chaos that actually allowed Jack to drift deeper into his own world, missing early opportunities to practice making contact.

His parents agreed on a set of routines that would bring Jack back into the mix of the family, giving him the chance to maintain consistent connections with the world outside his own. They began by setting up regular times for eating and sleeping as a family. At first Jack simply refused to play along. Jack's mother, a jovial, loud woman, was Fire natured and found it hard to relate to Jack, becoming easily overwhelmed by his detachment. His father was more Wood natured and yelled if Jack didn't cooperate, which of course Jack simply ignored. It took some time to reorganize his parents' habitual reactions in order to reduce the threat that led Jack to withdraw.

We realized that much of Jack's stubbornness came from having absolutely no sense of the passage of time, so I asked him and his parents to start playing The Time Game (see chapter 5). Timing his activities and logging them gave Jack a chance to connect to the passage of time in a more functional way. In doing so, he began to feel more connected to family routines.

Eventually Jack began to rely on his little stopwatch for timing everything, and this habit helped him map his day according to time rather than the infinite haze of Water contemplation. His mother started gently asking him when it was time for dinner or time to go to bed so that he became her helper. This strengthened their relationship and empowered him to help her stay with the routine too. Simply getting Jack on a daily routine changed his attitude, giving him more energy and making him less negative during the day.

The family began doing giant jigsaw puzzles at home. Jack loved the fact that these took weeks to complete, and working alongside his family helped him stay connected and focused on patterns. Jack also got better at playing cards with his brother, Freddie, a Wood child. As Jack got better at seeing patterns quickly, he began regularly winning, much to Freddie's dismay. We expanded his ability to identify patterns more quickly with many different games (see resources), and this changed the way he perceived things. Rather than going for the deep meaning, Jack learned to just pick up the lay of the land in order to get a sense of what he was looking at first. His parents used his interest in magic to expose him to science. They bought him a chemistry set for his birthday, and he and his father would spend hours together experimenting like two mad scientists.

I recommended that Jack begin Interactive Metronome therapy, a system that helps synchronize the timing of body movements (see resources). Out of this experience grew an interest in music, and Jack began playing piano the following year. He told me that whenever he felt stressed he could relax by playing the piano. The rhythm gave him a greater sense of security and honed his attention as well. Over time, Jack developed a very eclectic taste in music, ranging from R&B to jazz.

Training the Puppy Heart: The Power of Earth

Earth channels Water into the world. Its power lies in context and relationships. Training the puppy heart means using positive feedback to create opportunities for greater intimacy and engagement. One of Jack's great challenges was his seeming inability to connect with peers. He was unaware that he appeared odd and aloof. Other children would assume he wasn't interested in them, when in fact Jack desperately wanted to have friends. Feeling intimidated, Jack chose to retreat to his room and immerse himself in his reading. Starting slowly, he began having one-on-one playdates at his home with a classmate. This allowed him to practice sharing his secret world with another child. Earth powers relate to this kind of sharing. Developing a trusting relationship gave Jack added incentive to go to school and a greater sense of security when he got lost in the class. He'd simply look over to see what his friend was doing to get cues.

Eating on Planet Earth

Part of Jack's new family routine meant no longer eating in front of the TV, which had only made him more detached. Preparing meals and eating together began training Jack to take a more active role in the family. Jack would initially bring a book to the dinner table but rather than forcing him to stop, his parents encouraged him to tell them about what he was reading. This eventually developed into broader exchanges of ideas. This connection is a deeper meaning of mealtime. Jack and his father began developing their own story of a mythological hero, giving Jack something to look forward to at dinner. Experiencing their appreciation for his extraordinary imagination encouraged Jack to develop his storytelling skills, making connections between a character's actions and that character's feelings.

Being so immersed in his private world, Jack had often forgotten to eat. This is a perfect example of how a Water child gets disconnected from the basic rhythms of his body. Learning the meaning of hunger helps maintain fundamental neural connections important for learning. To improve this awareness, I taught him the I'm Hungry 1-2-3 Game (see chapter 5).

Breakfast was a particularly tricky meal for Jack. He was typically very sleepy and didn't feel like eating even if he'd had a good night's sleep. This difficulty in the morning worsened when he became a teen. I recommended that he start drinking a protein shake each morning. Jack preferred drinking caffeinated green tea, and I had to reassure his parents that this was one way to jump-start his Water mind. Sweets also helped stimulate him. While it's common to hear warnings that sweets are *never* good for the child with ADHD, the point of this book is to avoid making blanket statements about ADHD. "Less is more" means natural organic sweets (fruits and so on), which are of course preferred to unhealthy foods with added sugars.

Less Is Love

Jack's parents had initially found his natural detachment worrisome and frustrating. They had seen a psychiatrist who recommended starting him on antidepressant drugs, but his mother was scared off by reading all the warnings. Jack's parents had to be careful balancing his need to learn how to make contact with his need for privacy. Remember, less is love. Too much meddling only made Jack withdraw more. The balancing act began by making physical contact with Jack. Simply sitting by his side opened the possibility for eventual dialogue. But Jack's parents learned that they couldn't force Jack to talk about his problems. Pushing him only created more tension and withdrawal. Too much Earth muddies the Water. Jack's father discovered that simply reading in the same room offered just enough sense of connection to help Jack eventually make contact. Jack's mother was amazed to discover how effective taking long car rides together was in getting him to gradually share his thoughts.

EARTH MASSAGE

Making contact was crucial for directing Jack's attention back into the world. I taught Jack's mother a deep-massage technique that started at the bottom of his feet (Water points) and worked up the back of his legs and back, loosening muscles. Each night she put a drop of rosemary essential oil in warm water and moistened her hands before massaging (see appendix). Jack required a long time to get used to these massages, and his mother learned not to rush through them. In this case, the lesson of less is love meant less rushing.

Being an Earth Parent for Your Water Child

As caregivers, all parents are to some extent Earth natured. Imagine what it feels like to be a Water child whose power is to go deep, to immerse oneself in the mysteries of life. Now imagine the effect you are having if you invade that world too much. Imagine the insecurity your child feels when forced to make contact. Beware of your expectations of her. Try not to take personally your child's need to be alone. Explore the way your tone of voice and body language affects her behavior. Imagine how your child feels when you enter her world with love and care and share the adventure together. This opens the door to a true exchange of experiences.

Expanding the Big Heart: The Power of Wood

Just as spring comes out of the dead of winter, Wood is the natural outlet for Water. Wood represents action and movement. Jack's withdrawal was a call for help, a sign of his feelings of insecurity. Just getting Jack moving physically helped direct him back into the world. He began doing martial arts (Metal structure and Wood movement). His parents noticed almost immediately that this activity improved his attention to visual cues. They found that, over time, they didn't have to tell him over and over to do something. Once we were able to get him back in school, his teacher allowed him to do three jumping jacks whenever she saw him drifting off. We also started Jack walking every day to and from school. Initially he would arrive late to school. But eventually, with rewards, he learned to get better at judging his time.

Back to Nature

Although they lived in the city, Jack's parents began to make every effort to take walks in nature with him on weekends. In fact, they both loved this themselves. Expanding the big heart means gaining more experience with a diversity of feelings and sensations. Natural surroundings helped stimulate Jack's interests, making him more aware of his connection to the world around him. As his range of experiences expanded, so too did his ability to compare his feelings in different settings. Jack enrolled in a summer camp at a local nature preserve and he became fascinated with snakes and insects. In fact, it became a hot topic of conversation at our sessions together, being a wonderful outlet for him to connect with me and tell me all kinds of interesting facts. Gradually, Jack was able to make connections between his fantasy world and the adventures he had in nature. He loved playing a game in which we would talk about how characters in his beloved books might act in situations he had been in.

In Five Phase Correspondences, Wood power is connected to vision, the ability to see the path ahead. Around this time, I referred Jack for vision therapy, and he began wearing special prism glasses that made him look even more like a little professor (see behavioral optometry resources). He claimed that they helped him "see" in the classroom better.

Video Games and the Water Child

Digital technology may be highly addictive for many children, but not for *all* children. I find that it actually helps activate a Water child's attention. Studies have shown that video games can improve spatial awareness for some children (Spence and Feng 2010). While there is always the risk that a Water child might get lost in the gaming world, especially with so many online games that involve fantasy avatars, we found that planning twenty minutes of gaming activity before doing homework actually helped Jack prepare his mind for doing more mundane mental activities.

Mastering the Big Heart: The Power of Fire

Mastery comes with understanding how to use your powers wisely. For Jack, this meant first embracing his Water power, learning to train his attention outward and then recognizing the effect he was having on others. Fire represents fun, change, and enthusiasm. Jack gradually began to learn how his tendency to be cynical and negative put a damper on the fun around him. Learning how not to be a "downer" came from working in a social-skills group. Using his powers of introspection to reflect on his own behavior allowed him to practice adjusting his seriousness to circumstances. This was extremely challenging. He needed to first practice seeing through another's eyes.

Charades

Jack began playing charades with his family and then with friends. He learned to work in teams in which he had to adjust his body language in order to communicate with his partner. Jack's love for collecting cards for the game Magic: The Gathering got him interested in playing in local Magic tournaments with friends. These games explore a battle between wizards, and the fun lies in how well you work with team members. Realizing that these games involved a certain amount of luck lightened Jack's mood and helped him internalize the power of Fire. Though his parents were sometimes concerned about his deep immersion in these games, the interaction they brought was certainly better than him sitting alone in his room. (A note to parents: Water children's dark interests can lead them to potentially dangerous groups, especially now that there is such easy access to online communities. Parents must monitor this very closely.)

Singing Out

Fire and Water are on different ends of the spectrum. Water is dark and deep and very serious. Fire is light and bright and always changing. Getting Jack to cultivate a sense of Fire came with singing. His parents told me a story of how, once on vacation in Maine, they all sang around a campfire and it was "like he was a different kid, so happy, singing at the top of his lungs." As Jack got older, his interest in music became a wonderful way of igniting the Fire within. He joined a band and actually became the lead singer for a while, writing very profound songs that expressed his inner feelings. His mother loved the effect it had on Jack and told me how it shifted his mood and attention. He told me even listening to music on the way to school had an effect on his focus during the day, and he learned that certain styles of music made him more positive while others made him withdraw.

Developing this kind of sensitivity to his own shifting moods was extremely important to him. Over the years, he would come for acupuncture intermittently and we would take some time to practice meditations that opened him up to the creativity of his big heart.

Water Meditation

This meditation can be done sitting or lying down.

1. To begin, have your child do a few belly breaths. As she breathes in, her belly expands (not the chest). As she breathes out, her belly relaxes (letting go).

2. Now ask your child to imagine that she's the deep, blue sea, vast and filled with mystery. As she breathes into her belly, ask her to feel all the

streams running down from far-off snow-capped mountains, feeding her. Have her feel her weight expand while breathing in.

3. Breathing out, she'll let her breath rise up to the surface of the sea as waves. As she breathes in and out, ask her to try to let the waves grow still so that they can reflect the sun and sky above.

4. As she breathes in, ask her to silently give thanks to the mountain streams that make her so vast. Breathing out, guide her to give thanks to the sunlight that dances on the glass-like surface of her water.

Water Qigong Exercise: Standing Like the Sea

This exercise is best done before bed (facing north), but it can be practiced anytime to help calm the mind and prepare for sleep. It helps refresh the adrenal glands and kidneys.

1. Have your child stand with her legs separated as widely as is comfortable, feet flat on the ground. Ask her to imagine that she is the great ocean, whose currents run deep and wide.

2. As she faces straight forward, guide her to allow her gaze to focus on nothing in particular.

3. As she stands with her hands at her sides, have her breathe into her belly (see belly-breathing exercise, chapter 5) and raise her hands up over her head, palms facing forward. As she breathes out, have her gently bend forward and try to touch the inside of her ankles.

4. Breathing in again, she'll rise up slowly while sliding her hands up along her legs and around to grasp her lower back, fingers pointing down. Have her bend backward slightly; ask her to face the sky. She should hold and stretch slightly, but not strain. Ask her to try smiling and silently give thanks for the ground she stands on.

5. Now ask her to release her next breath while relaxing her body. As she breathes out, she'll come upright and gently bend forward once again, letting her arms drop and touching her ankles.

6. Start with one or two breaths and have her work her way up over the weeks. As she practices, guide her to focus only on her posture and the movement of her breath.

Homeopathy

Jack had an amazing response to homeopathy. Homeopathy involves extremely high dilutions of certain agents (Water power) that then neutralize specific symptoms. Though allopathic medicine does not accept this as valid therapy, it's certainly safe for children when prescribed by a knowledgeable professional. In Jack's case, a single dose of *Natrum muriaticum* had a tremendous effect on improving his mood and attention, and it became his constitutional remedy. I use homeopathy in many cases of ADHD. (See appendix for my Five Phase organization of homeopathic treatments for ADHD.)

Embracing Diversity: Becoming a True Sage in the World

Below are some activities parents, teachers, and therapists can work into homework assignments to help develop the Water child's strengths:

- Explain the meaning of the words "intuition," "light," and "love."

- Explain the meaning of the words "inspiration" and "original."

- Plan to do three random acts of kindness in one week.

- Give three examples of magic in the world.

- Read biographies of Houdini, Leonardo da Vinci, and/or Bob Dylan.

- Explore the magic of storytelling. Practice telling a story with lots of drama and expression.

- Study myths, legends, folktales, and parables and practice telling them to family.

Teaching the Water Child

School settings are often the biggest challenge for the Water child, and I find that Water children are often referred for special education services early because of their appearance of being "slow." A Water child's aloofness can be frustrating for any teacher who is trying to keep things moving. Finding a teacher who "gets" your Water-natured child can be a challenge. Often, Water children have missed the basic building blocks of learning and need to "relearn" the basics privately in order to catch up.

A teacher who can connect with the Water child's deeply personal interests can motivate her to stay engaged in class. Parents need to advocate for their child, making teachers aware of these unique interests. A Metal-natured teacher can provide the perfect structure to support your child's feelings of security and stimulate her love of scientific inquiry. However, this Metal needs to be like scaffolding that allows freedom to explore, not a cage. An Earth-natured teacher who isn't offended by the child who thinks outside the box will be able to include her in the group in a gentle and loving way. A Wood-natured teacher can be a wonderful role model, setting goals that keep your child moving forward. Fire-natured teachers can lighten the mood enough in the class to keep the Water child open and aware. Unfortunately, school may not be the ideal place for your Water child to thrive. I find that the best way for these children to learn is through apprenticeship. This is the way we humans learned for millennia, through one-on-one relationships. Alternative schooling is not always an option for parents but it can help support their child's self-esteem. Regardless of the style of teaching, what is of paramount importance in teaching your Water child is embracing her quirkiness while recognizing the immense effort necessary for her to fit in. Once self-esteem crashes, it can take a long time to coax her back out of her cave.

Jack Tuned In

Jack found meaning in his Water identity. It validated something he'd felt but had no way of explaining. Being told that his nature wasn't pathological was liberating for him. Over the years, we developed a solid therapeutic relationship. In helping him master his big heart, he recognized my deep respect for his inner wisdom and felt more confident. This feeling helped him to interact with the world. By putting his feelings into context, he gained greater perspective. In my office, we were able to joke about his absentmindedness as a sign of "too much Water" without it feeling threatening. By ninth grade, Jack had found a small group of boys who shared his eclectic interests. He began to volunteer at the social-skills class he'd been involved with. Working with younger kids gave him greater insight into his own earlier challenges and a broader perspective on how far he'd come from those early days. His grades have improved, and though his mother still complains that he's still a "space case" at times, she is genuinely proud of his progress. Jack has developed a passion for psychology, and his mother knows he's going to be an amazing therapist someday.

Here's a story about a Water teenager who discovered a way to be truly down to earth.

• *Sasha: A Water Teenager with ADHD*

I first consulted with Sasha when she was thirteen years old. She had recently become severely depressed and suicidal after being placed on stimulant medication for ADHD (inattentive type) by a psychiatrist. When Sasha was five years old, her mother, a single parent who was a teacher in a private school, already knew that she "wasn't like other kids." Sasha's mom feared that Sasha wouldn't be able to manage the institutional setting of public school. Sasha always took her own time doing things and, even as a one-year-old, had an amazing imagination and was content to live in her own world. She seemed to have a prodigious memory for music and a love of numbers. For kindergarten, Sasha's mother placed her in an alternative school that stressed hands-on learning. But by the second grade she could no longer afford private school and Sasha entered the public school system.

Sasha had never really shown an interest in other children and spent the next eight years as a loner, floating through school, staring out windows, and dreaming up little songs for herself. Her mother blamed the school for not getting Sasha interested in the subject matter and always tried to encourage Sashsa's unique talents for music and mathematics at home. She admitted that she'd often do Sasha's homework for her, just to help her keep up, but once Sasha entered middle school things fell apart. After countless meetings with the school, Sasha's mother finally agreed to bring her to a psychiatrist. Sasha was diagnosed with attention deficit disorder and prescribed a stimulant medication, which quickly caused such extreme reactions that Sasha stopped taking it. Sasha's mood had remained dark ever since, and her mother wouldn't even consider trying another medication. She came to me looking for alternative ways to help her child "survive the system."

As we talked about the five natures, I watched Sasha's mother's face light up when we got to the Water child. When I met separately with Sasha, she seemed to understand that she was a Water child even before I finished explaining all five natures to her.

In mapping out a solution for Sasha, we began by ensuring her sense of security by using Metal's power of pattern and routine. Simply acknowledging her unique Water nature within the pattern of the five had a powerful effect on both Sasha and her mother. Finally there was a context in which Sasha could be understood without attaching pathological labels, and this seemed to create some trust between us. Though her mom often joked that Sasha was a typcial "absent-minded professor," they both realized that Sasha needed to become more present-minded in order for her talents to shine in the world. I taught Sasha's mother to identify the telltale sign that Sasha's Water puppy heart was feeling insecure: increased withdrawal. Using the power of Metal meant developing a regular routine at home, which her mother (being Metal natured) took very seriously. Sasha also seemed to readily accept the fact that she needed more order to get her work done. Her mother created a schedule that they tried to stick to for homework, eating, and sleeping. This routine wasn't too confining and still allowed space for what Sasha called her "dream time." I encouraged Sasha to use her personal time to develop her love of music. She began to compose amazing little songs and poems of great depth that she would matter-of-factly bring to me on her visits.

Sasha started coming regularly for acupuncture. Because she was initially so afraid of needles (deep fears of the unknown are a common association with Water nature), we started by using tuning forks on acupuncture points to increase her awareness of her body. We could gauge her level of insecurity by how difficult it was for her to guess when the tuning forks had stopped ringing. This became very concrete evidence for her to measure her own level of stress. With patience, we were able to develop a trusting relationship (Earth) over the next few months. As a result, Sasha eventually allowed me to use acupuncture needles, which had a remarkable effect on her attention. Explaining my choice of acupuncture points intended for balancing Earth, Water, and Fire relationships helped her conceptualize the purpose of the treatment and reinforced her ability to focus on the changing sensations in her body rather than just idly daydreaming. Initially, she was actually unable to tell me whether the needles were in or out. However, as she got better at relaxing and focusing on her body sensations, it would take her less time to "warm up," as she called it. Within a few weeks, both her mom and her teachers recognized the difference in Sasha's attention. She seemed much more engaged in what was happening around her, and we built on this at each session by practicing shifting from mind to body. Recognizing these shifts helped Sasha feel more physically present in the world. I encouraged her to take a more active role in family activities whenever possible (Earth), and she was given responsibility for caring for the family dog, something she became passionate about (Fire).

Her grandparents owned a piece of land in the woods, and in the summer of her first year in high school, Sasha spent time working with her grandfather renovating their small cabin. This time in nature (Wood) became a wonderful outlet for her attention and

Sasha began planning visits whenever she could. Everyone noticed that she would return home feeling refreshed and more enthusiastic about life.

I referred her to a craniosacral osteopath (see resources) to promote greater internal balance and flow within her nervous system. Bones and marrow are associated with Water in Five Phase Correspondences, and this treatment seemed to improve Sasha's focus as well. She began taking Chinese herbs to strengthen Water in conjunction with herbs to support her adrenal glands (rhodiola, ashwaganda) when she was feeling particularly stressed (see resources). The amino acid l-tyrosine also helped get her attention stimulated in the morning.

By her junior year in high school, music had become an important part of Sasha's ongoing routine. She began taking piano lessons, which improved her attention to timing and rhythm (Metal). She quickly moved on to learn guitar and harmonica, and as she expanded her musical tastes she developed a passion for collecting and playing unusual instruments (Fire). That year, Sasha was invited to join a rock band, where for the first time she found genuine acceptance (Earth) for her quirky talent for songwriting.

When Sasha's grades once again began to suffer, we discovered that she had been getting lost in the vast world of the Internet. She was staying up late at night, immersed in the ocean of interesting information. Weaning her off her surfing habits required strict monitoring, and her mother again redirected her toward more physical activities.

Sasha also began to excel in math, which had always seemed to come easy for her. I recommended that she work more closely with the Math department at her school to develop these skills. The support and encouragement she found there helped support her self-esteem and offered a future direction for her life.

Sasha's struggle with attention was most noticeable when it came to writing. Though she could write a poem quite brilliantly, writing longer compositions in high school was a struggle. She had wonderful ideas but couldn't seem to get them down on the page. She would sit at her desk, staring at the page for hours. I recommended that she start recording her ideas first and then writing them down. Her mother would then help Sasha organize the material in sequence. Sasha actually began to enjoy the process of recording her voice, and this helped her public speaking as well.

Sasha loved talking with me about the five Chinese natures, and we even came up with an idea for a comic book. It featured five superheroes that represented the powers of the five natures, and perhaps one day this will become another book.

This year Sasha graduated from high school and is entering college. She'll be majoring in theoretical physics, though she told me that she'll be bringing all of her musical instruments just in case she decides to become a rock star.

Loving the Water Child

Think of your Water child as your guru, your little Yoda. Finding the humor in a Water child's quirkiness opens your heart and strengthens the bonds between you. Remember, it's hard to be a Water child in this crazy world of social relations. Deep Water connects us to the mystery of life. We cannot survive without water, just as a life without meaning feels empty. When a Water child is tuned in, she offers us an ocean of imagination, ideas that can revolutionize our world. Some of our most original thinkers were Water natured: Albert Einstein, Sigmund Freud, Leonardo da Vinci, and Buckminster Fuller, to name just a few. The Water child has something to offer us all. Her deep truths give purpose to Earth's context, nourish Wood's ingenuity, give meaning to Metal's patterns, and ground Fire's exuberance. Though the world is not always ready to hear her teachings, take the time to listen to the wisdom of your child. Be patient. She has some very profound things to teach you.

A Summary of the Approach to Water

- **Feeding the Puppy Heart:** Use the power of Metal to improve consistency and structure. Try The Time Game and Interactive Metronome.

- **Training the Puppy Heart:** The power of Earth means fostering attachments, taking social-skills classes, joining clubs, and eating together. Play the I'm Hungry 1-2-3 Game, prepare protein shakes for your child, and don't be afraid of a little caffeine for her.

- **Expanding the Big Heart:** The power of Wood includes physical movement, including walking meditations, hiking, martial arts, and yoga. Try vision therapy and allow limited video game use.

- **Mastering the Big Heart:** Cultivate the power of Fire with qigong exercises, meditation, games, singing, entertaining, homeopathy, craniosacral therapy, and storytelling.

Afterword

In reality, there is no single cure for ADHD because ADHD is not a single entity. We each go through the process of maturation and liberation in a unique way that is wholly dependent on the conditions in which we find ourselves. Laozi said it best: "Circumstances complete us" (author's translation). But rather than being mere victims of circumstance, our children teach us that we're unfinished business. In mapping your child's way, you're also mapping your own life. When you do so, you get a glimpse of the part you play in the great, mysterious ways of the universe: the Dao. Ultimately, this book is about the love that expands your big heart when you see your children find freedom from the things that hinder their growth. I hope that, through this book, you will discover your child's true nature and thus bring greater meaning and compassion to the circumstances you find yourself in.

Tidewinds, Brewster Dunes, MA
June, 2011

Appendix

Summary of Five Ways to Tune In and Tune Out

Big-Hearted: Tuning In to the Big Picture

Wood	Fire	Earth	Metal	Water
"The True Hero"	"The True Leader"	"The True Caregiver"	"The True Judge"	"The True Sage"
Attracted to movement	Attracted to novelty, sensation	Attracted to attachments	Attracted to order, detail	Attracted to deep meaning
Ambitious	Charismatic	Accommodating	Discriminating	Introspective
Loves exploring	Loves drama	Loves pleasing others	Loves logic	Loves theory
Goal-driven	Humorous	Loyal	Righteous	Imaginative
Learns by pushing boundaries	Learns by intuition	Learns by context and association	Learns by patterns and cause	Learns by deep inquiry
Decisive	Compassionate	Diplomatic	Ethical	Self-reflective
"In the flow"	"High engagement"	"Being present"	"Precision"	"Immersion"
Archetype: The Pioneer	Archetype: The Wizard	Archetype: The Peacemaker	Archetype: The Alchemist	Archetype: The Philosopher

©Stephen Cowan 2009

Barking Puppy: Tuning Out the World

Wood	Fire	Earth	Metal	Water
"The Wild Child"	**"The Class Clown"**	**"The Worrywart"**	**"The Stuck Child"**	**"The Daydreamer"**
Distracted by stillness	Distracted by boredom	Distracted by separation	Distracted by disorder	Distracted by ideas
Fights constraint	Impulsive	Anxious	Rigid	Withdrawn
Easy frustration	Easy meltdowns	Disorganized	Hyperfocused	Apathetic
Hyperactive	Overstimulated	Indecisive	Self-righteous	Stubborn
Hostile	Panicky	Obsessive thinking	Compulsive	Depressed
Shouting	Sensory overloaded	Meddlesome	Disappointed	Dread
Tension headaches	Hypoglycemia	Bruising	Constipation	Malaise, fatigue
Muscle twitching	Reflux	Stomachaches	Eczema, asthma	Back pain
Numbness	Diarrhea	Muscle weakness	Tics	Hypochondria

©Stephen Cowan 2009

Five Phase Aromatherapy

Essential oils can be used in baths, vaporization, or massage (mixed with sunflower oil or lotions).

Wood	Fire	Earth	Metal	Water
Hyperactivity/Tension headache	**Impulsivity/ Oversensitivity/ Diarrhea**	**Anxiety/Stomachache due to worry**	**Hyperfocusing/ Rigidity/Constipation**	**Apathy/Backache**
Bergamot	Geranium	Chamomile	Frankincense	Basil
Chamomile	Ginger	Cinnamon	Geranium	Clary-sage
Cumin	Lavender	Fennel	Jasmine	Geranium
Frankincense	Mandarin	Ginger	Lavender	Mandarin
Lavender	Neroli	Lime	Orange	Pine
Lemon	Rose otto	Mandarin	Tangerine	Rose otto
Peppermint	Spearmint	Peppermint	Yarrow	Rosemary
Ylang ylang	Sandalwood	Rosewood		
	Vetiver			
	Yang yang			

©Stephen Cowan 2009

Five Phase Flower Essences

Wood	Fire	Earth	Metal	Water
Peppermint Mental tension	**Indian Pink** Sensory overload	**Cosmos** Excessive thoughts	**Filaree** Hyperfocus on details	**Clematis** Excessive daydreaming
Lavender Tension	**Madia** Inattention to detail	**Pink Yarrow** Blurring boundaries	**Shasta Daisy** Inability to see the big picture	**Queen Anne's Lace** Lack of presence
Overstimulation	**White chestnut** Overactive mind	**Walnut** Indecisiveness	**Honeysuckle** Negative outlook	**Rosemary** Feeling disembodied
Cedarwood Lack of focus	**Saint-John's-wort** Hyperstimulation	**Wild oat** Confusion in making decisions	**Borage** Discouragement	**Forget-Me-Not** Loneliness and isolation
Vetiver Anxiety	Panic	**Mountain Pride** Worry	**Lavender** Tension	
Hyperactivity		Can't stick to goals	Hyperfocus that interrupts sleep	
Rabbitbrush Mental rigidity			**Cayenne** Mental stagnation	
Mental dullness			**Nasturtium** Hard-edged thinking	
			Zinnia Overseriousness	

Five Phase Homeopathy

Wood	Fire	Earth	Metal	Water
Tuberculinum	*Medorrhinum*	*Calc carbonica*	*Cina*	*Natrum muriaticum*
Never satisfied	Extreme extrovert	Plodding	Oppositional	Withdrawn
Restless	Fails to finish	Forgetful	Stubborn	Negative
Irritable	Forgetful	Sweaty	Irritable	Low motivation
Destructive	Excessive masturbation	Overweight	Picks at self	Clumsy when hurried
Bed-wetting	Fears being alone	*Baryta carbonica*	Itchy nose	Cries in private
Tarantula	*Plantago*	Forgetful	Resents interference	Cold sores
Overactive	Hurried	Touchy	Muscle twitches	Craves salt/pasta
Impulsive	Reflux	Separation anxiety	Hypersensitive head	*Scorpion*
Climbs like spider	No perseverance	Craves ice	*Aurum metalicum*	Lacks compassion
Motor tics	Hypersensitive	*Lachesis*	Easy disappointed	Detached
Impulsive	Impulsive	Excessive talk	Grief	Likes to be alone
Chamomilla	*Capsicum*	Left-sided symptoms	Sobs in sleep	Indifferent
Frenzied	Sluggish	Jealousy	Noise sensitive	Isolated
Rage	Overweight	*Veratrum album*	Depressed	*Silica*
Restless	Red cheeks	Busy	Frequent colds	Shy
"the ungoverned child"	Hypersensitive	Chatterbox	*Arsenicum album*	Timid
Lyssin	Homesick	Worrier	High strung	Chilly
Fits of rage				

Stramonium				
Fear of dogs	Fears of dark	Restless	Frightened	Sickly
Claustrophobia	Stutter	Craves ice, cold foods	Delicate	Skin problems
Impulse to cut oneself	Cursing		Despair	
Bedwetting	Jealousy		Dislikes mess	
			Hoarseness	
			Asthma	
			Cold sensitive	
			Hypersensitive	

©Stephen Cowan 2011

Five Phase Foods General Guidelines

Wood (sour) (so)	Fire (bitter) (bb)	Earth (sweet) (sw)		Metal (pungent) (pp)	Water (salty) (st)
Wheat	Corn	Millet	Eggplant	Rice	Buckwheat
Nuts	Rye	Sweet potato,	Potato	Chicken	Salt
Hawthorne	Red lentil	yam	Squash, yam	Spearmint	Egg
Artichoke	Alfalfa	Chickpea	Almond	Rosemary	Fish
Broccoli	Romaine lettuce	Malted syrup	Coconut	Radish (bb)	Seaweed
Vinegar (bb)	(sw)	Cherry	Tomato (so)	Scallion (bb)	Barley, millet (sw)
Apple (sw)	Asparagus	Date	Apple	Garlic	Soy sauce
Blackberry	Arugula	Fig	Banana	Onion	Miso
(sw)	Scallion (pp)	Beet	Cantaloupe	Cinnamon	Pickle (so)
Raspberry	Endive	Carrot (so)	Mango	Cloves	Sesame salt
(sw)	Escarole	Cucumber	Papaya	Ginger	Olive (so)
Sauerkraut	Vinegar (so)			Cabbage	Beet
Carrot (sw)	Apricot			Cauliflower	Kale
Rhubarb	Guava			Celery	Mushroom
Grape (sw)	Loquat			Cucumber (sw)	Water chestnut
Avocado	Raspberry			Leek (so)	
Olive (st)	Strawberry			Watercress	
Lemon					
Tomato (sw)					
Lime					
Orange					
Pickle (st)					
Rose hip					

©Stephen Cowan 2011

Adapted from Garvy 1985 and Pitchford 2002

(Note: There is great disagreement among experts regarding food classifications. Foods are complex mixtures, just like people. Some foods share more than one phase designation. Please use this only as a guideline.)

Resources for Caregivers

There are excellent links available at my website: www.stephencowanmd.com
    Below are a number of exceptional resources I have found helpful for parents.

Body Work and Meditation

yogakids.com

Yoga for Anxiety: Meditations and Practices for Calming the Body and Mind (2010) by Mary NurrieStearns, LCSW, and Rick NurrieStearns.

Buddha's Brain: The Practical Neuroscience of Happiness, Love, and Wisdom (2009) by Rick Hanson, PhD, and Richard Mendius, MD.

Teaching Meditation to Children: A Practical Guide to the Use and Benefits of Meditation Techniques (2000) by David Fontana and Ingrid Slack.

Chinese Pediatric Massage Therapy: A Parent's and Practitioner's Guide to the Treatment and Prevention of Childhood Disease (1999) by Fan Ya-Li.

ataonline.com (American Taekwondo Association)

www.aikidoglobal.com

Power Animal Frolics: Tai Chi/Yoga/Qigong for Children (2008) DVD Directed by Saba Moor-Doucette.

Dietary Advice

There are a number of excellent websites that offer parents information about healthy food. "Two Angry Moms" is a movement I have been involved in to help change the quality of food in schools.

angrymoms.org

nalusda.gov/afsic/csa (community-supported agriculture)

www.ewg.org/foodnews (downloadable guide to pesticide contamination of fruits and veggies)

www.ams.usda.gov/farmersmarkets (a national listing of farmer's markets)

Superimmunity for Kids: What to Feed Your Children to Keep Them Healthy Now and Prevent Disease in the Future (1989) by Leo Galland, MD (one of the first books written about the importance of DHA omega-3 in children's health)

Supplements and Herbal Remedies

I use a number of supplements in children to help promote healthy attention. Please consult with a licensed practitioner before giving your child any supplements.

designsforhealth.com

www.metagenics.com

xymogen.com

Chinese Herbs for Children

I treat children using a number of Chinese herbs. Efrem Korngold developed a great line of herbs called "Gentle Warriors" for the Kan Herb Company. Please consult a licensed practitioner before giving herbs to your children.

kanherb.com

Flower Essences

Dr. Edward Bach developed the first series of flower essences in the 1930s as a radical departure from conventional medicine at the time. Basing his work on the field of homeopathy, one of his important contributions to alternative medicine was to consider the emotional roots of all disease. These dilutions are very safe when used correctly and can be effective for a number of physical and mental problems. Please read instructions on application of remedies carefully before using.

Bach Flower Remedies for Children: A Parents' Guide (1997) by Barbara Mazzarella.

bachflower.com/children.htm

flowersociety.org/

Aromatherapy

These books are great resources for parents. Please consult with a professional before using any oil.

Aromatherapy for the Healthy Child: More than 300 Natural, Nontoxic, and Fragrant Essential Oils (2000) by Valerie Ann Worwood.

Aromatherapy for Babies and Children (1996) by Shirley Price and Penny Price.

Homeopathy

These resources offer parents a guide to choosing the right homeopathic medicine for their child's condition.

www.boiron.com

Homeopathic Medicine For Children and Infants (1992) by Dana Ullman.

The Spirit of Homeopathic Medicines: Essential Insights to 300 Remedies (1997) by Didier Grandgeorge, MD.

Analogy and Pattern

Analogy Adventure (1989) by Linda Schwartz and Beverly Armstrong.

Advancing through Analogies (1992) by Dianne Draze and Lynne Chatham.

The Book of Patterns (2011) by Hervé Tullet.

Mind Games: Pattern Games (2001) by Ivan Moscovich.

www.zoodles.com
Free online games for kids. See pattern recognition games.

Adjunct Therapies that Help Attention

interactivemetronome.com

heartmathstore.com (resource for buying the portable emWave device, which can be used at home to synchronize heart rate and respiration)

Transforming Stress: The HeartMath Solution for Relieving Worry, Fatigue, and Tension (2005) by Doc Childre and Deborah Rozman, PhD.

Neurofeedback resources. While it is best to consult with a trained specialist in neurofeedback, these resources offer computer-based programs that children can use at home.

www.playattention.com

www.wilddivine.com

Sensory-integration therapy resources. Occupational therapists are often trained in providing sensory-integration therapy. Here are a few resources that offer more information that may be useful for improving your child's attention.

www.sensory-processing-disorder.com

The Out-of-Sync Child: Recognizing and Coping with Sensory Processing Disorder (2006) by Carol Kranowitz.

spdfoundation.net

Behavioral optometry. *The Suddenly Successful Student: A Parents' and Teachers' Guide to Behavior and Learning Problems and How Behavioral Optometry Helps* (1986) by Ellis Edelman.

Craniosacral osteopathy. This gentle therapy can be useful in adjusting subtle disharmonies in the circulation of fluid in the nervous system.

cranialacademy.com

Craniosacral Therapy for Babies and Small Children (2006) by Etienne Peirsman and Neeto Peirsman.

Your Inner Physician and You (1997) by John E. Upledger.

Home Organization

The Emotional House: How Redesigning Your Home Can Change Your Life (2005) by Kathryn L. Robyn and Dawn Ritchie.

Other Books on ADHD

The Gift of ADHD (second edition, 2010) by Lara Honos-Webb, PhD.

The Edison Gene: ADHD and the Gift of the Hunter Child (2005) by Thom Hartmann.

Last Child in the Woods: Saving Our Children from Nature-Deficit Disorder (2008) by Richard Louv.

Scattered: How Attention Deficit Disorder Originates and What You Can Do about It (2000) by Gabor Maté.

References

Ainsworth, M., M. Blehar, E. Waters, and S. Wall. 1978. *Patterns of Attachment*. Hillsdale, NJ: Erlbaum

American Psychiatric Association. 2000. *Diagnostic and Statistical Manual of Mental Disorders (DSM-IV-TR)*, 4th edition. Washington, DC: American Psychiatric Association.

Andersen, S. L., and M.H. Teicher. 2009. Desperately driven and no brakes: Developmental stress exposure and subsequent risk for substance abuse. *Neuroscience and Biobehavioral Reviews* 33(4):516-524.

Baumeister, H., and M. Härter. 2007. Mental disorders in patients with obesity in comparison with healthy probands. *International Journal of Obesity* 31:1155-1164.

Beinfield, H., and E. Korngold. 1992. *Between Heaven and Earth: A Guide to Chinese Medicine*. Ballantine Books

Blunden, S.L., C.M. Milte, and N. Sinn. 2011. Diet and sleep in children with attention deficit hyperactivity disorder: Preliminary data in Australian children. *Journal of Child Health Care* 15(1):14-24.

Charlton J.P., and I.D.W. Danforth. 2007. Distinguishing addiction and high engagement in the context of online game playing. *Computers in Human Behavior* 23(3):1531-1548.

Center for Disease Control Data and Statistics on Attention Deficit Disorder. 2007. http://www.cdc.gov/ncbddd/adhd/data.html

Cohen, K. 1997. *The Way of Qigong.* New York: Ballantine.

Edebol, H., A. Kjellgren, S. Bood, and T. Norlander. 2009. Enhanced independence and quality of life through treatment with flotation-restricted environmental stimulation technique of a patient with both attention deficit hyperactivity disorder and asperger syndrome: A case report. *Cases Journal* 2:6979.

Farr, S.A., W.A. Banks, and J.E. Morley. 2006. Effects of leptin on memory processing. *Peptides* 27(6):1420-1425.

Garvy, J.W. 1985. *The Five Phases of Food: How to Begin.* Newtonville, MA: Wellbeing Books.

Gómez-Pinilla, F. 2008. Brain foods: the effects of nutrients on brain function. *Nature Reviews Neuroscience* 9:568-578.

Granet D.B., C.F. Gomi, R. Ventura, and A. Miller-Scholte. 2005. The relationship between convergence insufficiency and ADHD. *Strabismus* 13(4):163-168.

Hinshaw, S.P., and S.M. Melnick. 1995. Peer relationships in boys with attention-deficit hyperactivity disorder with and without comorbid aggression. *Development and Psychopathology*, 7:627-647.

Johnson, S.L. 2000. Improving preschooler's self-regulation of energy intake. *Pediatrics* 106:1429-1435.

Jung-Beeman, M., E.M. Bowden, J. Haberman, J.L. Frymiare, S. Arambel-Liu, R. Greenblatt, P.J. Reber, and J. Kounios. 2004. Neural activity when people solve verbal problems with insight. *PLoS Biology* 2(4):0500-0510.

Kim, Y., M. Teylan, M. Baron, A. Sands, A. Nairn, and P. Greengard. 2009. Methylphenidate-induced dendritic spine formation and ΔFosB expression in nucleus accumbens. *Proceedings of the National Academy of Sciences* 106 (8): 2915-2920.

Kleinman, R.E., S. Hall, H. Green, D. Korzec-Ramirez, K. Patton, M.E. Pagano, and J.M. Murphy. 2002. Diet, breakfast, and academic performance in children. *Annals of Nutrition Metabolism* 46(1): 24-30.

Kraus de Camargo, O. 2010. The international classification of functioning, disability and health (ICF): An ideal framework for developmental-behavioral pediatrics. *Section of Developmental and Behavioral Pediatrics Newsletter* 20:11-13.

Kuo, F.E., and A.F. Taylor. 2004. A potential natural treatment for attention-deficit/hyperactivity disorder: Evidence from a national study. *American Journal of Public Health* 94(9):1580-1586.

Lam L.T., and L. Yang. 2007. Overweight/obesity and attention deficit and hyperactivity disorder tendency among adolescents in China. *International Journal of Obesity* 31(4):584-590.

Lin, L. 2009. Breadth-biased versus focused cognitive control in media multi-tasking behaviors. *Proceedings of the National Academy of Sciences* 106(37):15521-15522.

Lloyd A., D. Brett, and K. Wesnes. 2010. Coherence training in children with attention deficit hyperactivity disorder: Cognitive functions and behavioral changes. *Alternative Therapies in Health and Medicine* 16(4): 34-45.

MacLean, P.D. 1973. A triune concept of the brain and behavior. In The Hincks Memorial Lectures, T.J. Boag and D. Campbell, editors, pages 6-66. Toronto: University of Toronto Press.

MacLean, P. 1985. Brain evolution relating to family, play, and the separation call. *Archives of General Psychiatry* 42(4): 402-417.

Mannuzza S., R. Klein, H. Abikoff, and J. Moulton. 2004. Significance of childhood conduct problems to later conduct disorders among children with ADHD: a prospective followup study. *Journal of Abnormal Child Psychology* 32 (5): 565-573.

Marazziti, D., A. Del Debbio, I. Roncaglia, C. Bianchi, A. Piccinni, and L. Dell'Osso. 2008. Neurotrophins and attachment. *Clinical Neuropsychiatry* 5(2):100-106.

Mathiak, K., and R. Weber. 2006. Toward brain correlates of natural behavior: *f*MRI during violent video games. *Human Brain Mapping* 27(12): 948-956.

Mattson, M.P. 2008. Dietary factors, hormesis and health. *Ageing Research Reviews* 7(1): 43-48.

Mattson, M.P., and Calabrese, E.J. 2010. Hormesis: What it is and why it matters. In *Hormesis: A revolution in biology, toxicology and medicine*, M.P. Mattson and E.J. Calabrese, editors, pages 1-14. New York: Humana Press.

McCraty, R., and D. Childre. 2010. Coherence: bridging personal, social and global health. *Alternative Therapies in Health and Medicine* 16(4):10-24.

Moffitt, T.E., L. Arseneault, D. Belsky, N. Dickson, R.J. Hancox, H. Harrington, R. Houts, R. Poulton, B.W. Roberts, S. Ross, M.R. Sears, W.M. Thomson, and A. Caspi. 2011. A gradient of childhood self-control predicts health, wealth, and public safety. *Proceedings of the National Academy of Sciences* 108(7): 2693-2698.

National Institutes of Health. 1998. *Diagnosis and Treatment of Attention Deficit Hyperactivity Disorder.* NIH Consensus Statement. 16(2): 1-37.

Ophir, E., C. Nass, A.D. Wagner. 2009. Cognitive control in media multitaskers. *Proceedings of the National Academy of Sciences* 106(37): 15583-15587.

Osher, Y., Y. Bersudsky, and R.H. Belmaker. 2005. Omega-3 eicosapentaenoic acid in bipolar depression: report of a small open-label study. *Journal of Clinical Psychiatry* 66:103-112.

Oshi, K., S. Lad, M. Kale, B. Patwardhan, S.P.Mahadik, B. Patni, A. Chaudhary, S. Bhave, and A. Pandit. 2006. Supplementation with flax oil and vitamin c improves the outcome of attention deficit hyperactivity disorder (ADHD). *Prostaglandins Leukotrienes and Essential Fatty Acids* 74:17-21.

Parker, G., N.A. Gibson, H. Brotchie, G. Heruc, A. Rees, and D. Hadzi-Pavlovic. 2006. Omega-3 fatty acids and mood disorders. *American Journal of Psychiatry* 163: 969-978.

Parker, S., S. Greer, and B. Zuckerman. 1988. Double jeopardy: the impact of poverty on early child development. *Pediatric Clinics of North America* 35(6): 1227-1240.

Pitchford, P. 2002. *Healing with Whole Foods: Asian Traditions and Modern Nutrition.* Berkeley, CA: North Atlantic Books.

Rubinstein, J.S., D.E. Meyer, and J.E. Evans. 2001. Executive control of cognitive processes in task switching. *Journal of Experimental Psychology: Human Perception and Performance* 27(4): 763-797.

Sagan, C. 1980. Cosmos. New York: Ballantine.

Seah, M., and P. Cairns. 2008. From immersion to addiction in videogames. *British Computer Society* 1: 55-63.

Selye, H. 1978. *The Stress of Life,* 2nd ed. New York: McGraw-Hill.

Shaw, P., K. Eckstrand, W. Sharp, J. Blumenthal, J. P. Lerch, D. Greenstein, L. Clasen, A. Evans, J. Giedd, and J. L. Rapoport. 2007. Attention-deficit/hyperactivity disorder is characterized by a delay in cortical maturation. *Proceedings of the National Academy of Sciences* 104 (49): 19649-54.

Sibley, B., R.M. Ward, T. Yazvac, K. Zullig, and J.A. Potteiger. 2008. Making the grade with diet and exercise. *AASA Journal of Scholarship and Practice* 5(2): 38-45.

Sinn, N. 2007. Polyunsaturated fatty acid supplementation for ADHD symptoms: Response to commentary. *Journal of Developmental and Behavioral Pediatrics* 28(3): 262-263.

Sinn, N., and J. Bryan. 2007. Effect of supplementation with polyunsaturated fatty acids and micronutrients on learning and behavior problems associated with child ADHD. *Journal of Developmental & Behavioural Pediatrics* 28(2): 82-91.

Sobczak, S., A. Honig, A. Christophe, M. Maes, R.W. Heldingen, S.A. De Vriese, and W.J. Riedel. 2004. Lower high-density lipoprotein cholesterol and increased omega-6 polyunsaturated fatty acids in first-degree relatives of bipolar patients. *Psychological Medicine* 34(1): 103-112.

Soh, N., G. Walter, and C. Collins. 2009. Nutrition, mood and behavior: A review. *Acta Neuropsychiatrica* 21(5): 214-227.

Spence, I., and J. Feng. 2010. Video games and spatial cognition. Review of General Psychology 14(2): 92-104.

Su, K.P., S.Y. Huang, C.C. Chiu, and W.W. Shen. 2003. Omega-3 fatty acids in major depressive disorder. A preliminary double-blind, placebo-controlled trial. *European Neuropsychopharmacology* 13(4): 267-271.

Swing, E.L., D.A. Gentile, C.A. Anderson, and D.A. Walsh. 2010. Television and video game exposure and the development of attention problems. *Pediatrics* 126(2): 214-221.

Taheri, S., L. Lin, D. Austin, T. Young, and E. Mignot. 2004. Short sleep duration is associated with reduced leptin, elevated ghrelin, and increased body mass index. *PLoS Medicine* 1: 210-217.

Tang, Y., Q. Lu, X. Geng, E.A. Stein, Y. Yang, and M.I. Posner. 2010. Short-term meditation induces white matter changes in the anterior cingulate. *Proceedings of the National Academy of Sciences* 107(35): 15649-15652.

Tang, Y., Y. Ma, J. Wang, Y. Fan, S. Feng, Q. Lu, Q. Yu, D. Sui, M.K. Rothbart, M. Fan, and M.I. Posner. 2007. Short-term meditation training improves attention and self-regulation. *Proceedings of the National Academy of Sciences* 104(43):17152-17156.

Tang, Y., Y. Ma, Y. Fan, H. Feng, J. Wang, S. Feng, Q. Lu, B. Hu, Y. Lin, J. Li, Y. Zhang, Y. Wang, L. Zhou, and M. Fan. 2009. Central and autonomic nervous system interaction is altered by short-term meditation. *Proceedings of the National Academy of Sciences* 106(22): 8865-8870.

Weatherholt, T.N., R.C. Harris, B.M. Burns, and C. Clement. 2006. Analysis of attention and analogical reasoning in children of poverty. *Journal of Applied Developmental Psychology* 27(2): 125-135.

Wesnes, K.A., C. Pincock, D. Richardson, G. Helm, and S. Hails. 2003. Breakfast reduces declines in attention and memory over the morning in schoolchildren. *Appetite* 41(3): 329-331.

Zito, J., D. Safer, S. dosReis, J. Gardner, M. Boles, and F. Lynch. 2000. Trends in the prescribing of psychotropic medications in preschoolers. JAMA 2883 (8): 1025-1030

Stephen Scott Cowan, MD, is a board-certified pediatrician specializing in holistic developmental pediatrics who has over twenty years of experience working with children and families. He is a fellow in the American Academy of Pediatrics, a member of the AAP section on developmental disabilities, a member of the American Academy of Medical Acupuncture, and a clinical faculty member at New York Medical College. He has lectured internationally and currently practices in New York.

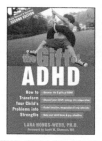

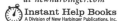